# The Orange Flash of Freedom: Understanding and using the Bitcoin Lightning network

Juraj Bednár

Written and produced in 2024 by Juraj Bednár
I don't care about copyrights. Enjoy the book and be excellent to each other.

# Table of contents

INTRODUCTION  9

START WITH A SIMPLE LIGHTNING WALLET – PHOENIX OR BREEZ  12

    User view  13

    Phoenix installation and setup  14

    Installation and setup of Breez  27

    Differences between Breez and Phoenix  32

    Conclusion  34

WHAT ARE PAYMENT CHANNELS?  35

    Bi-directional operation  41

    Bitcoin blockchain as a dispute resolver  43

    From a payment channel to a payment network  47

    Channel capacity  54

    Security  62

    How to back up Lightning  63

MYTHS AND DIFFERENCES BETWEEN LIGHTNING AND BITCOIN ON-CHAIN  67

    Are Lightning Bitcoins real Bitcoins?  67

| | |
|---|---|
| Lightning has no addresses | 70 |
| Lightning has no history | 72 |
| Finality - transactions are confirmed immediately | 73 |
| Fees | 74 |
| **LIGHTNING ECOSYSTEM** | **76** |
| Wallets | 77 |
| Accepting Lightning payments at premises | 88 |
| **USABILITY AND USAGE OF LIGHTNING NETWORK** | **90** |
| **LIGHTNING AND PRIVACY** | **93** |
| **ON-CHAIN PRIVACY USING LIGHTNING** | **98** |
| Accepting on-chain payments with privacy | 98 |
| Watch out for correlations using amounts | 101 |
| Lightning or coinjoin? | 102 |
| On-chain with Phoenix and Breez | 103 |
| **MUTINY WALLET** | **106** |
| Desktop version | 106 |
| Mutiny on a mobile device as a Progressive Web App | 118 |
| Progressive Web Application (PWA) and subscription option | 123 |
| Conclusion | 126 |

## ZEUS: THE MOST FLEXIBLE MOBILE LIGHTNING WALLET?     127

### Connecting Zeus wallet to your own node     129

### Lightning node on the device     131

### Accepting payments     136

### Sending sats     139

### Channel Management     140

### Settings     143

### Point of sale – accepting payments     145

### Conclusion     152

## EXPANDING THE LIGHTNING NETWORK TO SERVE BILLIONS – A QUICK-WIN STRATEGY     154

### Expanding Lightning     155

### Using Liquid to expand Lightning     156

### Advantages for users     158

### Advantages for merchants     158

### Advantages for wallet providers     159

### Advantages for Bitcoin and Lightning     159

### How to do it?     159

### Why not Litecoin, …?     160

### But isn't it custodial?     160

| | |
|---|---|
| How does it work in practice? | 163 |
| Conclusion | 165 |

## LIGHTNING NETWORK – THE PAYMENT NETWORK OF THE INTERNET — 166

| | |
|---|---|
| Lightning is the ideal payment protocol | 167 |
| Searching for the ideal payment protocol of the internet | 168 |
| Liquidity | 168 |
| Absence of dirty coins | 169 |
| Programmability | 169 |
| Even better programmability | 172 |
| Second generation backend software | 174 |
| Conclusion | 175 |

## CONCLUSION — 177

## BONUS: BITCOIN IN A HIGH FEE ENVIRONMENT — 179

| | |
|---|---|
| What are the current fees? | 180 |
| I sent a transaction with too low a fee and it is unconfirmed for a long time | 184 |
| Double spend, Replace by Fee | 185 |
| Child pays for parent | 188 |
| Transaction Accelerator | 191 |

| | |
|---|---|
| Lightning network | 191 |
| Custodial lightning | 194 |
| Uncle Jim | 196 |
| Non-custodial wallet | 198 |
| Permanent node | 199 |
| When are Lightning payments worth it? | 201 |
| Liquid | 202 |
| Ecash - Cashu and Fedimint | 204 |
| Uncle Jim running an ecash mint | 206 |
| Several Uncle Jim's | 209 |
| Conclusion | 210 |

# Introduction

Bitcoin has created a native internet digital decentralized scarcity. It's a protocol that allows us to have something that is digital but cannot be copied by replicating of the bits that make up that information. What's more, it's created in a decentralized way. It's the first project that has all the properties mentioned - no central authority, scarcity, and it's a native Internet protocol.

However, Bitcoin itself is not a very good payment network from several perspectives. Every transaction is verified by all nodes of the network. The Bitcoin "timechain" (or "blockchain") is a very inefficient decentralized database that has just one unique property - it allows the creation of a decentralized cryptocurrency. The Lightning network was created to address these issues: efficiency, speed and cost of the transactions. And as a bonus, it has better privacy than Bitcoin's public database.

Lightning uses Bitcoin as a unit of account and an asset in a direct and decentralized manner, but unlike the classic "on-chain" transactions as we know them from the original Bitcoin protocol, it uses a different mechanism to send satoshis (or sats, the smallest units of Bitcoin, like cents to a dollar).

However, the Lightning network uses the Bitcoin protocol to resolve "disputes". This means that we communicate with counterparties we may not trust, and in the event of a fraud attempt, the Bitcoin network will "decide" the dispute in the favor of the side that did not try cheating.

Precisely because of this, Bitcoin used in a Lightning channel is not a IOU (I owe you) of Bitcoin, but Bitcoin itself. You can always, without a third party get the Bitcoins you are supposed to own.

This is where we get a bit confusing terminology, because we use the word Bitcoin to refer to several things - a unit of account, a payment network, a peer to peer communication network, and software (which has since been called "Bitcoin Core" instead).

Lightning replaces both the peer to peer communication network (how nodes talk to each other) and the payment network (how payments are done), but uses Bitcoin itself as the unit of account - not even just its accounting representation, but Bitcoin itself, which we'll explain further in the book.

The Lightning network is thus a payment network that uses Bitcoin as the unit of account and is backed by real Bitcoins. You connect to the network by creating so-called payment channels through which you can send Bitcoins to the network and receive Bitcoins from the network.

You don't need to have an open payment channel with someone to send them Bitcoins - just like when you have an Internet connection from your ISP, you don't have a direct fiber-optic cable from your home going to the datacenter where Amazon (or me) has their servers, but you can still order this book. The provider has a connection to the peering center, there is another provider connected there that provides connectivity to the datacenter and so over multiple "cables" you connect to the server which you want to connect to. Thanks to digital signatures within the HTTPS protocol, we can even ensure that the communication between your device and the server cannot be altered by anyone - this feature is also key with the Lightning network.

Throughout this short book, I will explain how the Lightning network works, what are payment channels, what wallets can we use and how to accept Lightning payments in your store or business. We will talk about solutions in high fee situations and look deeply in some of the projects.

Before we start with the explanation of Lightning and how it works, I'll introduce one of the simplest (but still non-custodial) wallets – Phoenix Wallet, which you can install as you read to try things out. I have been recommending Phoenix as the only Bitcoin wallet, as it does Lightning and on-chain well and has a unified balance.

# Start with a simple lightning wallet – Phoenix or Breez

I believe that the best way to learn is through experience. I used to say that I can explain Bitcoin either by doing a two hour talk, or just showing you in five minutes. If you follow along this, you will end up with a Bitcoin and Lightning wallet that works, is self-sovereign (you own the keys) and does not require identity verification.

Lightning wallets have historically had a reputation for being like rocket science. The user had to run their own node, open channels, and make complex configuration settings. The "solution" to this problem of complexity, which is still presented as the best by many bitcoiners as of today, is to use a "custodial" wallet - that is, to make Bitcoin not an self-sovereign electronic cash system, but turn it into a bank account with QR codes. Fortunately, this whole looking at Lightning is outdated - the Breez and Phoenix wallets show that it is possible to have a wallet that keeps the sovereignty of the users over their assets (i.e., private keys), but automatically and reasonably well handles all the other tricky stuff - node, network connectivity, routing, channel creation, and even switching between on-chain and lightning.

I know that I did not explain these concepts in detail yet, but that's the beauty of these wallets – in order to use them, you do not have to understand anything yet. But don't worry, we'll explain it later.

## User view

Both wallets can be used right away with a few clicks after installation. You can accept your first Bitcoins either via Lightning or using on-chain payments. Both wallets will create a Lightning channel when you make your first payment. Unlike many other wallets (Zeus, Mutiny, Aqua, Blixt, Green) you have one balance - all your Bitcoins are in a Lightning payment channel. From the user's perspective this is very convenient, they don't have to move Bitcoins between two payment networks.

Where these wallets differ is the overall concept. Breez is a laboratory of Lightning technology and is built as a "super-app", like China's WeChat. In Breez, you can listen to podcasts (and stream sats to your favorite podcasters thanks to podcasting 2.0 technology). It has a few other apps integrated that are available directly from the Apps menu, where you can directly access services like Bitrefill, Wavlake, Boltz, Azteco or The Bitcoin Company. Breez also works as a point-of-sale terminal to accept payments on the fly.

In contrast, the Phoenix app is extremely simple - it does one thing and does it well. It can receive and send Bitcoin payments - whether on-chain or via Lightning. In fact, there are a few interesting other features under the hood, but the effort is clearly to create a minimalist Lightning wallet that just works.

## Phoenix installation and setup

First, let's look at the Phoenix wallet setup. Once installed from the stores (Play or App Store, depending on the platform), we are greeted by a splash screen. We can then choose whether we want to create a new wallet or restore a backup:

*Image: initial selection - do you want to create a wallet or restore another Phoenix wallet from seed?*

If we click to create a new wallet, we can start using it immediately:

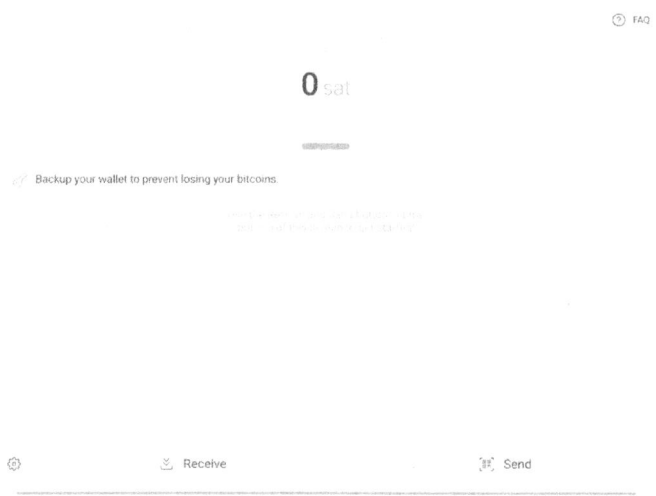

The whole wallet is about two buttons - Receive and Send. Note that the wallet notifies us that we haven't backed it up yet, we should not forget to do that (I'll show you how later).

That was easy, wasn't it? It's even easier than custodial wallets - no need to fill in any email addresses or phone numbers. Now let's accept the first payment. Let's click on the Receive button.

After clicking on Receive, a QR code will pop up, but before that you will see information that the first payment will include a fee. In this case, the fee is 2984 sats. If the fees are higher than usual, we will need to change the settings and increase the maximum fees we are willing to pay by clicking on Configure fee limit. These fees are largely based on how many transactions are waiting to be confirmed on the bitcoin network and we will talk about how fees work later in the book.

After dismissing the fee screen, we can click on the Edit button and write a description of the incoming payment (this description will also be seen by the sender and will remain in your wallet as a description of the payment) and the amount you want from the other party. You can enter the amount in sats, but also in your chosen fiat currency (you can choose this in the settings).

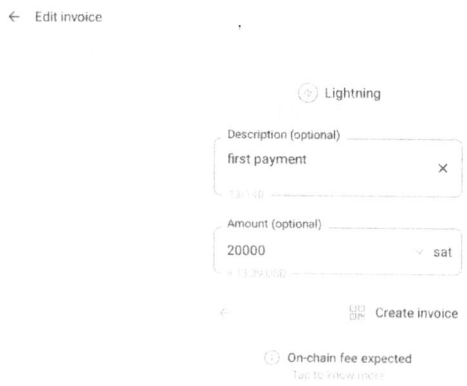

After entering a description and amount, you can click on Create Invoice. The application still warns us that we need to make an on-chain transaction (in this case, opening a channel) to receive this amount and thus we should expect a fee.

When you click on Create Invoice, the app will display the QR code of the Lightning Invoice. However, we can also share the invoice (by clicking the share button) or copy it to the clipboard.

If we pay this invoice from another wallet, we will get a confirmation screen:

RECEIVED just now

+17,782 sat

first payment

SERVICE FEE  1,000 sat
MINER FEE   1,218 sat

Received payment will show how much we have received in the wallet and what is the fee breakdown – we have paid 1218 sats to the miners and 1000 sats as a service fee for first opening of the channel.

The received payment has no confirmations on the network, the channel funding transaction has to be included in the block (mined) by the miner. However, since the payment came via Lightning the balance is immediately usable and we don't have to wait for the miners at all.

Sending works in a similar way - click on the Send
button. After enabling access to the camera (so we
can scan QR codes), we can either scan the QR
code from the display of recipient wallet, or insert
a payment request from the clipboard. I scan the
QR code from my BTCPayServer:

However we give the wallet the payment request
(lightning invoice), the next screen will give us the
details - payment description, amount, fees and so
on.

←                          17,782 sat

10051 sat
≈ 6.73 USD

Paid to Juraj Bednar (Order ID: )
02f1246b8fe904a5c5193504d80695
32b1fb8692b84fb3eb64318b20123...
44 sat

Pay

We can look at the main screen where we can see an overview of all payments and access other settings, including the ability to request liquidity.

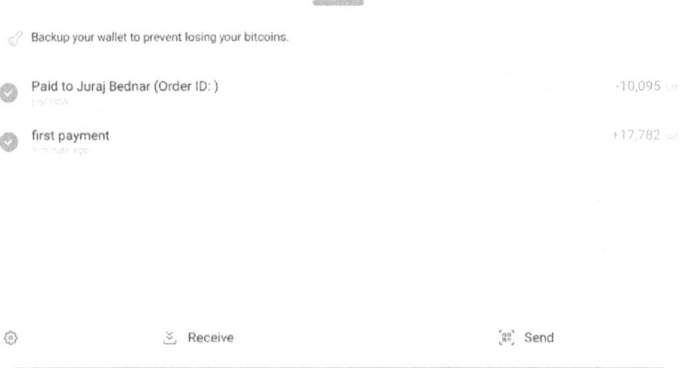

By clicking on "sat" after the balance (7,686 sat) on top, we can change the currency in which the amounts are displayed - for example, to Euros, Dollars, Czech Crowns, Paraguayan Guarani or any other fiat currency. With another click, we can also hide the balances so that we don't show the wallet balance when we interact with other people.

On the screen, I hope we all noticed that we still haven't backed up our wallet. Let's fix that - clicking on the warning will take us directly to the backup screen. If we'd like to backup again later, pressing the gear button on the bottom left will take us to the settings menu and we can select "Recovery Phrase".

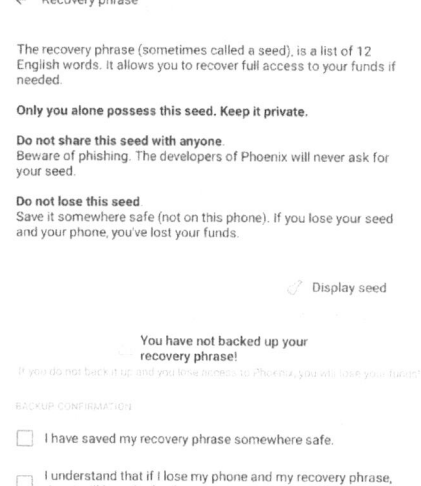

The backup page is self-explanatory, I recommend reading it carefully. Clicking on "Display seed" will show us 12 words to write down.

After writing down the 12 English words that make up the wallet's backup, we confirm that we have written them down in a safe place and that we understand that if we lose both our phone and our backup, we will never get our Bitcoins back.

Please, really make a proper paper backup and store it somewhere safe. Please don't just take a screenshot stored randomly in your photos library. And by the way, the wallet won't allow you to do a screenshot anyway, although many people "solve" this by taking a picture of their phone with the camera on their other phone. A lot of people lost money because they wanted to make a backup "sometime later". It's 12 words, you write it down in less than three minutes.

To accept on-chain Bitcoin, swipe left in the Receive tab - this will display the Bitcoin address and its corresponding QR code. Simply send Bitcoins to this address and they will appear in your wallet. You don't need to do anything special to send an on-chain payment - if you scan the on-chain address or payment request (or paste it from the clipboard), the payment will normally work as if you were using a normal Bitcoin on-chain wallet.

Let's look at a few more interesting settings. Click on the gear wheel to display the menu:

← Settings

GENERAL

⊘ About

𝒫 Display

𝒫 Payment options

⚙ Channel management

≡ Payment history

🔔 Notifications

PRIVACY & SECURITY

🔒 Access control

𝒫 Recovery phrase

⊘ Electrum server

🛡 Tor

If you are into privacy, you can turn on the Tor anonymization network. Phoenix (unlike Breez) has Tor support directly integrated in the wallet and all we need to do to use it is to turn it on in the menu. It's good to say here that using Phoenix with Tor is significantly slower, all payments may not go through automatically, and the app occasionally needs to be restarted to connect to a different Tor entry point. Personally, I use Phoenix without Tor.

In the Display section we have the option to change the fiat currency, language and display settings.

← Display options

**Bitcoin unit**
Satoshi (sat)

**Fiat currency**
 USD

**Application theme**
Follow system

**Application language**
English

If we know that we will be using the wallet more for receiving payments than spending, we may want to request liquidity. We do this by clicking the "Request Liquidity" button on the main screen.

If you want to increase incoming liquidity, it is a good idea to do that when on-chain fees are low (usually weekends), so that we don't pay too much to the miners. At the same time, higher liquidity is often cheaper in percentage fees - while the payment to Phoenix Wallet liquidity provider depends on the amount (1% at the time of writing), the miner fee is fixed, so you can get more liquidity for the same fixed miner fee and don't have to extend it later.

If you want to see the use of the Phoenix wallet on video, I recommend the first lesson of the course A quick introduction to Bitcoin – wallet setup, buying, payments. The course is available for free and without registration.

Find it at:

https://hackyourself.io/bitcoin-intro

## Installation and setup of Breez

The installation and setup of Breez works very similarly. The app is also controlled by two buttons, Send and Receive, although there is a special button for scanning QR codes, located between these buttons. This is because with a QR code we can not only send, but also receive (thanks to the lnurl standard) and also login to some web-sites.

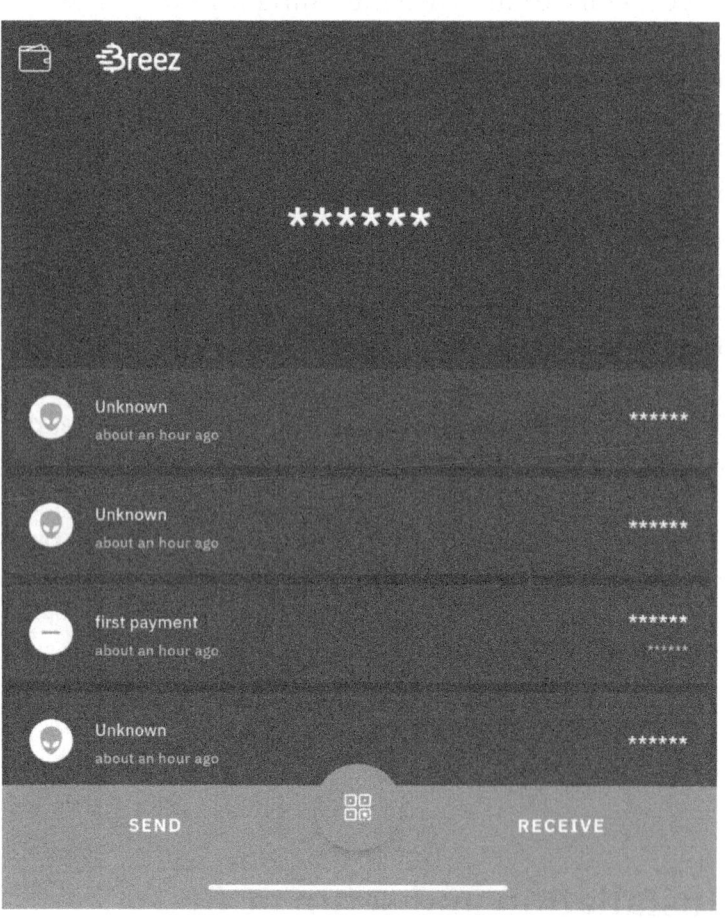

Both Phoenix and Breez have this login functionality, thanks to support for the LNURL-Auth protocol, which you can use to log in to some services with your Lightning wallet. It's useful because you don't need a traditional email address or password, and the Lightning Wallet backup is also a backup of your login credentials. In addition, you don't have to worry about sites identifying you, or cross-matching you with each other - the login is unique to the domain and has no relation to any other login elsewhere, not even to payments. This makes it easy for you to log in without having to create any accounts via email addresses and write down passwords. If you have a backed up wallet, you also have a backup of your accounts.

Precisely because we can use QR code scanning to send, as well as receive or log in to websites, Breez has a special button for scanning QR codes. In the Phoenix wallet, it's also possible to receive and log in using a QR code, but we can access this functionality somewhat counter-intuitively via the "Send" button that launches the QR code scanner.

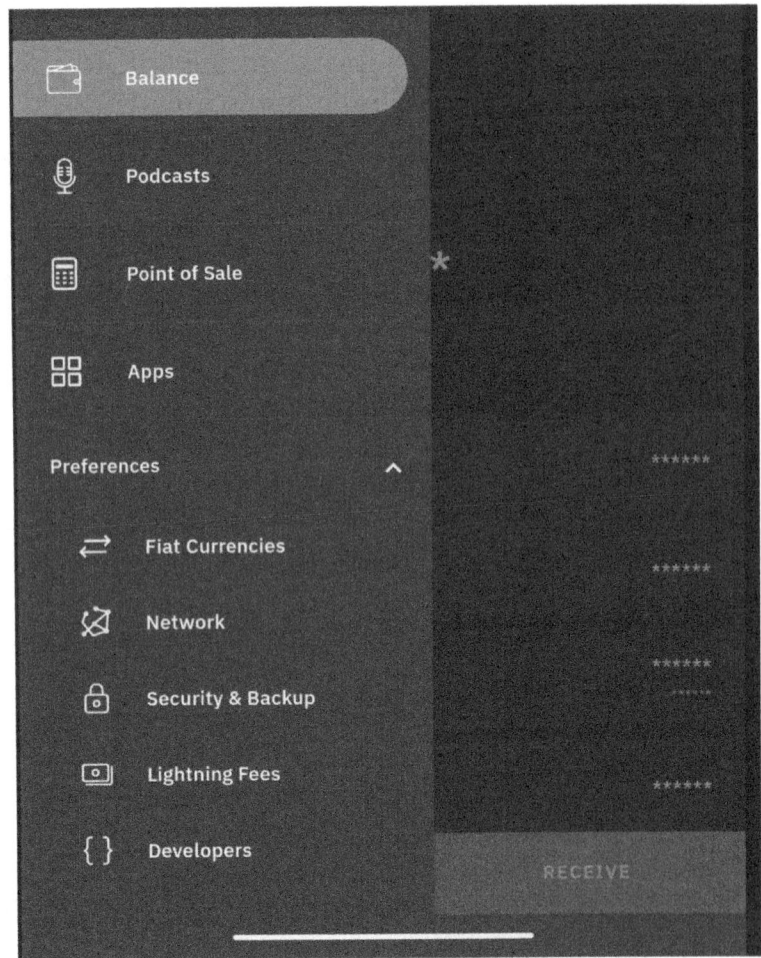

*Image: menu with settings and options. You'll find a podcast player, Point of Sale module, and access to Lightning apps from the wider lightning ecosystem.*

In the settings menu you will find, besides the fiat currency display setting, also an important menu with a backup. Unlike Phoenix, Breez doesn't store backups on the server of the wallet provider, but allows you to save the backup to your cloud account. Supported cloud providers are Google Drive on Android and Apple iCloud on iOS. However, you can also use your own server (for example, NextCloud) using the webdav protocol. The backup is in the form of an encrypted file (encryption must be specifically enabled in the settings).

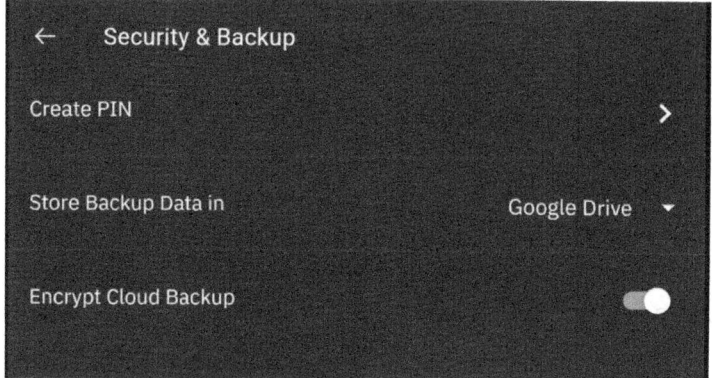

*Image: Backup settings. You can store your backup with different cloud providers, of course I recommend turning on encryption.*

You can restore the backup either in Breez wallet or using the standard lnd installation. Breez is in fact a full lnd node running on your phone.

# Differences between Breez and Phoenix

Phoenix runs a minimalist node on your device that just signs new channel states based on payments. Everything related to your channel balance is handled directly by your app, but almost everything else is done by a smarter server that has visibility into the channels of the network and can therefore find the payment path faster and easier. Therefore, the payment speed is basically the same as with custodial wallets (i.e. fast).

Breez by contrast runs a full lnd node on your device – this node does everything. It needs to sync with the Bitcoin blockchai, and it also needs to download information about the connected nodes in the network so that it can find payment paths locally on the device (we will explain what this means later).

This has two drawbacks - it can be slow and data-intensive to start up (don't do it over a limited data plan – either first time or after not using it for a long time), and also the payments themselves are slower and can fail more often. With Breez, it's better to open the wallet from time to time and allow it to update your network view.

The advantage with Breez is significantly higher privacy. The liquidity service provider (which is directly Breez in this case) sees the payments going through, but doesn't know directly who you are paying. The end-to-end payment path is created by your device.

Breez supports listening to podcasts with sat streaming, directly logs you into various apps, and even allows you to accept lightning payments in your establishment.

See the video demonstration of how Breez works as a point of sale for accepting Lightning payments:

https://hackyourself.io/breez-pos

The video is part of the course "Lightning network for private bitcoin payments among friends and for products and services", which you can find at https://hackyourself.io/shop

Of course, you can receive payments in your establishment also using Phoenix, when you request liquidity, but in the case of Breez, you can set a "manager password" that is required to send payments. So you can use the device in use to receive payments, but even if the device is stolen, you won't lose Bitcoins because an additional password is required to send.

# Conclusion

Both Phoenix and the Breez are great wallets for beginners. Thanks to them, hopefully most new users will skip the custodial wallet phase and take their private keys into their own hands. I personally find Phoenix to be a good bitcoin wallet for both lightning and on-chain transactions for complete beginners. The success rate of payments is huge, the wallet works fast and reliably. The user doesn't have to deal with whether to use Lightning or on-chain, as both experiences are perfectly integrated.

The Breez wallet is for more patient users – the wallet needs to synchronize the block headers, figure out the topology of the Lightning network for routing, and so on. This makes the wallet significantly slower, and the success rate of payments is a bit lower. On the other hand, it contains a lot of interesting functionality - PoS terminal, podcast player with value4value functionality, or easily accessible Lightning apps. Swapping to Lightning is also an advantage with fairly good privacy (see a later chapter on this).

In conclusion, I wish you would try at least one of these wallets and offer them to newbies instead of custodial wallets. I think the best Phoenix.

Now let's look at payment channels.

# What are payment channels?

Now that we have shown how to use Lightning practically, let's talk about how Lightning works. Lightning is made out of payment channels.

The payment channel is a special Bitcoin address (or, for advanced users, actually a UTXO) where Bitcoins are locked. The channel is always between two network users, let's call them Alice and Bob.

Alice sells great gluten-free pancakes and Bob loves them and wants to buy them regularly for the whole family for dinner. Since he wants to pay with Bitcoin every time and doesn't want to pay the Bitcoin on-chain fee every day, it would be great if he could pay just one such fee and then spend that money repeatedly at Alice's.

*Image: Alice makes pancakes and Bob pays her with hard money (Bitcoin), but he doesn't want to burden the network with an on-chain transaction every time.*

A simple channel might look like Bob sending Alice and advance payment and subscribing to ten dinners. The problem is that if Bob's family does not want to eat pancakes anymore, or the quality drops, or a new pancake restaurant appears, which Bob prefers to Alice, a rather awkward situation arises where Bob has to go to Alice and ask her to return the unspent portion of the balance back in the form of hard money. And an even more awkward situation happens when he learns that Alice has already spent the money. Bob doesn't have a private key to this money, he has already sent it to Alice and so Alice has to sign a transaction to return the difference.

However, the payment channel for Alice's pancakes may look different. Alice remembered that Bitcoin allows for 2-for-2 multisig, in which each transaction must be signed by both parties.

She proposes this solution to Bob: "together we create an address from which we can only spend together". Bob, after they agree on which keys will control that address (one key and thus signature for Alice, one for Bob), will send the amount for ten pancake dinners (called a funding transaction). Before he signs and sends this transaction to the network though, he tells Alice that he wants a signature on another transaction that will send all the Bob's money from the funding transaction straight back to Bob. This other transaction is called a commitment transaction.

However, Bob merely saves this commitment transaction and does not send it to the Bitcoin network - so if Alice goes bankrupt or Bob does not want to eat any more pancakes, Bob takes the transaction signed by Alice, adds his signature to it, and immediately gets all his "credit" back.

*Picture: the channel between Alice and the bob. It has a capacity of 10 dinners and they all belong to Bob for now.*

Bob buys the first dinner and agrees with Alice that now the price of one dinner out of the total amount for 10 dinners goes to Alice, and Bob gets the balance for nine dinners. They exchange a new signed commitment transaction that would split the money this way - one dinner to Alice at her Bitcoin address, nine dinners to Bob at his Bitcoin address. But they don't send this transaction to the Bitcoin network either, they just set it aside. If Bob starts going to a competitor and doesn't show up for a long time, Alice can send this transaction to the Bitcoin network, the miner will mine it, and she gets her Bitcoins for one dinner (and Bob automatically gets the remaining money). Bob can do the same thing at any time - Alice goes bankrupt and can't be contacted, Bob takes the last signed transaction and sends it to the network, the miner mines it, and Alice gets her money for one dinner and Bob gets his nine.

Of course, now you're saying to yourself - what if Bob cheats and sends the first commitment transaction that Alice signed for him at the beginning, getting money for all ten dinners. For this purpose, payment channels have what are called revocation keys. These are exchanged between the parties when signing a new transaction. If Bob used this old transaction, Alice would take her revocation key and take all the money (for all ten dinners). A penalty transaction is a penalty for sending a status older than the last one. Thus, no one has to worry about any fraud (that's the "judging disputes using the Bitcoin network" feature). The last signed transaction reflects the current payment status and just needs to be communicated to the miners. Any older transaction sent to the network means that the defrauded party can take all the Bitcoins from the channel.

(Technical detail: to make this work the network uses a trick that the transactions that each party puts off don't look the same. Alice has a transaction where the price of nine dinners goes to Bob right away, but the price of one dinner goes to Alice only after a certain amount of time, at which point Bob has the opportunity to use the revocation key. Thus, if Alice sends the transaction to the network, Bob gets his money right away, but Alice has to wait to see if Bob has a revocation key to take the price of one dinner. Bob has Alice sign exactly the opposite transaction - Alice gets her money for one dinner right away, but Bob has to wait to see if Alice has a revocation key - after the time lock expires, Bob can take the money, Alice can take all the money with the revocation key).

## Bi-directional operation

Alice and Bob are normally able to account for who owes how much to whom on their own. They have a payment channel in which all the money belongs to Bob at the beginning, and gradually as Bob pays for the dinners, more and more of the money goes to Alice. If Alice discovers that Bob is selling coconut oil, which Alice can use to fry pancakes, Alice can also send money back to Bob. Not right away, however, because once the channel is opened, all the money belongs to Bob and Alice gets her balance only with the dinner payments. If Alice wanted to buy coconut oil right after opening a channel, she would have to open another one and "charge" it with her Bitcoins, or make other arrangements with Bob - for example, she can send money to Bob using an on-chain payment, and in return Bob sends money through the channel to Alice, which Alice can spend. The operation in order to allow both parties to send and receive equally through the channel is called channel rebalancing or channel centering. It can also be done in various other ways. Alice and Bob can even agree to both put Bitcoins in the channel. Opening the channel in this way is called "dual funding".

It is important to know that Bitcoins can be sent both ways through the channel, as long as there is a sufficient balance on that side. You can think of it as an abacus.

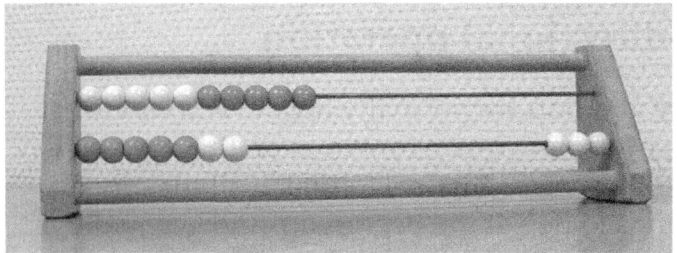

*Abacus. Used under Creative Commons license. Created by Onderwijsgek from nl.wikipedia.*

The payment channel is a single row abacus. At the beginning, the entire capacity is on Bob's side. Bob can send some marbles to Alice's side and thus the balance of ten marbles is split between them - one marble belongs to Alice, nine belong to Bob. Alice can only send the marbles she has on her side. If she wants to send more, she must open a new payment channel.

# Bitcoin blockchain as a dispute resolver

The point of the payment channel is that once it is created by a Bitcoin on chain transaction to the 2-of-2 mutlisig address (called a funding transaction), there can already be infinitely many transactions between Alice and Bob (within the capacity of the channel). Said marbles can move left and right as their owners please. No one in the Bitcoin network has any idea what the balance is on which side, and neither Alice nor Bob pay any Bitcoin fees to the miners. At any point in time, both Alice and Bob have a valid signed transaction that can send the current Bitcoin balance to their addresses. This is the equivalent of "having the keys".

A common Bitcoin saying is "not your keys, not your Bitcoins". Alice and Bob don't have to trust each other. If there is a dispute, it will be resolved by the Bitcoin blockchain, because at any point in time they can both send a valid signed transaction that fairly divides the Bitcoins between Alice and Bob as they are due.

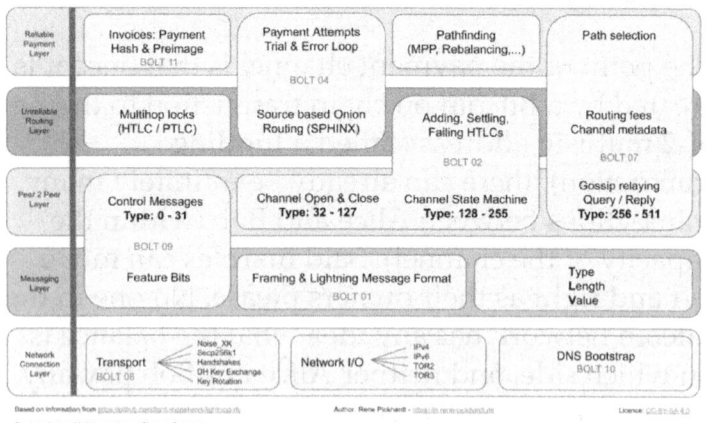

*Figure: Schematic of the protocols that make up the Lightning network. This is a fairly complex payment network, part of which is directly mapped to Bitcoin's protocols, and so dispute resolution is provided. Source: René Pickhardt, CC BY-SA 4.0 via Wikimedia Commons*

The argument doesn't have to be just about Alice and Bob having a fight or trying to cheat each other. For example, Alice's Internet connection might go down, Bob gets a little nervous that Alice isn't communicating, and decides he'd rather keep his bitcoins in his on-chain wallet. He already doesn't care much about using the channel with Alice, since she's not communicating anyway, he can't make or receive any more payments through that channel. He can choose to send the last state of the channel to the bitcoin network. It's like having a "backup" of the state of the abacus in the form of a Bitcoin transaction. This transaction is a fairly ordinary, valid Bitcoin transaction, signed by both Alice and Bob, and it distributes the bitcoins according to the last state to Alice and Bob.

However, Bob may be a con artist and when he notices Alice isn't responding, he may send an old state – an old signed transaction. However, the Bitcoin blockchain can also resolve this dispute - Alice will come online within a few days and take all of Bob's money (including money that would otherwise belong to him) as a penalty for wanting to cheat. But what if Alice can't make it because she's really offline? That's what the watchtowers in Lightning network are for. They keep track of old states and send a penalty transaction to the network for Alice even in her absence if someone sends an old state. This is safe because the penalty transaction is also signed and can do nothing but penalize the sending of the old state. If no one sends the old state to the network, it doesn't do anything - it's invalid in the same way as if someone wanted to spend bitcoins they don't have.

# From a payment channel to a payment network

I do not need to have a direct channel open with the recipient of the payment in order to make a payment through the Lightning network. This is possible thanks to payment paths. Charlie the masseur also buys pancakes from Alice. He also buys coconut oil from Bob for oil massages. Both Charlie and Bob have a channel with Alice, but Bob and Charlie do not have a direct channel between them. How can they (financially) communicate with each other?

If Charlie sends Alice payment for one coconut oil and asks her to forward it to Bob, it's easy. However, a problem arises if Alice takes the payment (Charlie signs her new channel state), but does not tell Bob about the payment - that is, if Alice does not update the channel state she has with Bob. If the payment network operated on trust, it wouldn't be that useful. Fortunately, we don't have to trust Alice.

Bob sends Charlie a Lightning invoice (for example a QR code on an actual invoice). The invoice includes not only the amount for the oil, a description or the expiration ("due time"), but also the so-called payment hash. This is a part of a key that unlocks the payment.

Let's look at this invoice:

lnbc10u1pjl5qjnpp5q359ssfmzw72l9ap5un4ydu8vwxw
jd52zhtf5grnwkx24chc9ghsdqqcqzpuxqyz5vqsp5pzhk
w89pwtk6936jye9pguwffph9trktz2wzay9awzsztdl0p49
s9qyyssqq47pg0rprrswpj5r9n2cywj6x9682hl9v7tdmfpq
clsfw0j09nxxzvt7znz6y3nxuchgyvsw94kjzt0vrqx9uxw
enl3k84ng492yt0sqhljmv9

It can be represented also as a QR code:

Feel free to scan it with a Lightning wallet, it has already expired by the time you read this, so it is not possible to pay it.

The information contained in this string is the following:

```
Chain: bitcoin (Lightning network also works
on other cryptocurrencies, such as Litecoin,
but it is only widely used on Bitcoin)

Amount (Millisatoshis): 1000000 (that is
equivalent to 1000 satoshis, Lightning is
```

partially ready for the time when 1 BTC equals 100 million dollars and you want to be able to send less than one Satoshi, which would be equivalent of 1 dollar in this case)

Payee Pub Key:
**02fcc5bfc48e83f06c04483a2985e1c390cb0f35058b aa875ad2053858b8e80dbd**

Transaction Signature:
**057c143c6118e0e0ca832cd5823a5a3174755fe56796 dda420c7e0973e4f2ccc61317e14c5a24666e62e8232 0e2d6d212dec180c5e19d99fe363d668a95445be** (these are key materials and signature that tie the invoice to a particular Lightning node – for additional verification that you are paying the right recipient the right amount. Note, that this identity can be totally random and one-time only, if the recipient wishes for more privacy)

Payment Hash:
**046858413b13bcaf97a1a727523787638ce9368a15d6 9a2073758caae2f82a2f** (giving a "prehash" to this payment hash unlocks this payment, allowing the nodes along the route to take the payment – I will explain this later)

Description: -- (sadly this invoice does not have description, but it can be any text that tells both sides what the payment was about – it is communicated only between the sender and the recipient)

Minimum Final CLTV Expiry: 60
Expire Time: 86400

Expiration: 2024-03-20T21:23:31.000Z
Timestamp (issued): 2024-03-19T21:23:31.000Z

As we can see, this invoice was valid for 24 hours starting 19th March 2024 at 21:23:31

Now back to our example. Charlie asks Alice to forward the payment, but instead of sending her the payment he asks her to adjust the channel status as follows:

- If a predetermined amount of time passes (e.g. 15 minutes), the money in the amount of the invoice remains with Charlie
- If Alice receives a "preimage" whose hash matches the hash on the invoice (explained in more detail later), the payment is "unlocked" and that part of the channel goes to Alice.
- All other parts of the channel belong to the original owners.

Alice has no reason not to sign such a distribution - either she will have as much money as before or, if she somehow gets "preimage", she will have more money.

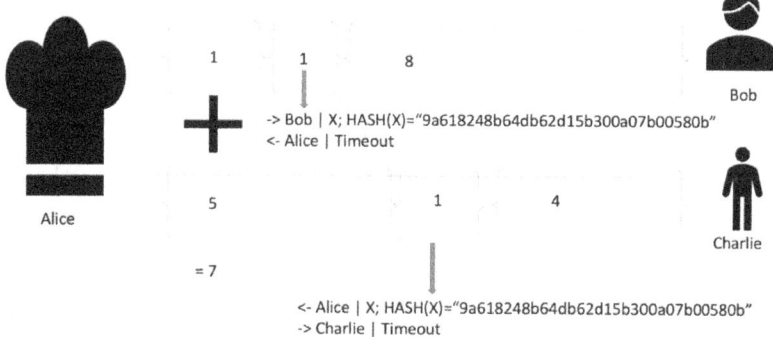

*Image: Charlie sends money to Bob via Alice. The payment is made by Charlie creating a path based on the hash from Bob's invoice. Bob confirms the payment by passing Alice a preimage (X) whose hash matches the hash in the created path. He can then take satoshis from the channel with Alice, and Alice can take satoshis from the channel she has with Bob.*

In order for Alice to gain the preimage she must ask for a similar setup in her channel towards Bob. She sends Bob money if she gets the preimage, otherwise the money stays hers. Alice is willing to sign this transaction because, although she will have less money in the channel with Bob, the same preimage can be used immediately to get money from Charlie, so she will not lose or gain anything, only her channel state will change - she will have more in the channel from Charlie, less in the channel from Bob.

Bob sees that he can get the money for the payment from Charlie. All he has to do is send Alice a preimage. This automatically unlocks the money for him. Alice sends this preimage to Charlie and gets the money on her side. If the channel state has stabilized, the preimage can be deleted from the transactions and the channel will revert to the original abacus like channel - splitting the funds between the two sides of the channel.

I know this part might be a bit too dynamic for reading, so here's a video overview:

https://hackyourself.io/lightningvideo

Alice, of course, prefers to make pancakes rather than sign transactions, which is why fees play a role in all of this. In order for Alice to find time to sign transactions in between flipping pancakes, it would be nice if she got a little more from Charlie than she sends to Bob. This is the fee for routing the payment. This fee is earned by Alice, not the miner, because such a payment is not sent to the Bitcoin blockchain at all.

The Bitcoin blockchain, even in the case of a payment passing through multiple payment channels, only arbitrates disputes, and it is possible to determine at any moment how much money belongs to which party. Even if a channel closes during a payment, everything is fine - the other channels through which the payment passed are unaffected and there is never a direct on-chain transaction between Bob and Charlie.

In this whole simple market exchange, ideally there are only two on-chain transactions - the opening of a channel between Alice and Bob and the opening of a channel between Alice and Charlie. All sales of pancakes, coconut oil and massages in this small ecosystem already take place outside the Bitcoin blockchain, are settled instantly (no need to wait for confirmations) and with minimal fees. Furthermore, these transactions are only handled by communication between the parties involved - no one else will know about these payments.

Bitcoin on-chain transactions "burden" the whole world (as they have to be validated and stored by all the nodes), but Lightning payments are private and take place as "whispers" between Alice, Bob and Charlie. Together, they are able to come to an agreement, and if a problem arises, they only resolve the dispute with the problematic party - by sending the last valid transaction to the Bitcoin blockchain.

# Channel capacity

If you open a channel, you can usually only send satoshi through that channel. However, some wallets handle this by adding "their" Bitcoins to their side of the capacity if you open a channel, so they have something to send you through that channel. You can then both receive and send. Another option is to send some of the money back on-chain using a swap service such as Breez, or Boltz once the channel is open. You pay a lightning invoice through that channel, and by paying that invoice, the provider sends the balance (minus fees) back to you on-chain. In this case you end up with a larger channel where some of the capacity is on your side.

How to think about channel capacity? There are more analogies, let's try to use this one:

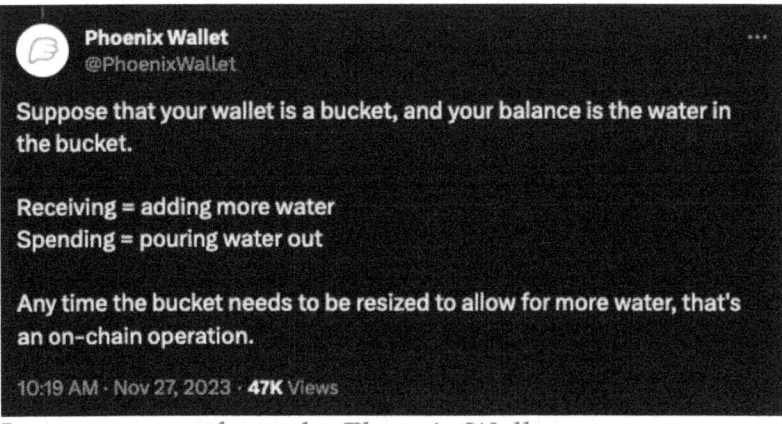

Image: a [tweet from the Phoenix Wallet account](#) about how to think about channel capacity.

Imagine your wallet is a bucket and your balance is water in the bucket. If you pay with water, you pour the water out (into another container, for example). Receiving is pouring water into your bucket. You can always "spend" (pour out) the water you have in your bucket. But if you want to take in (pour in) more water than you have free space in your bucket, you need a new bucket.

Whenever it is necessary to change the size of the bucket in order to pour more water into it, it is an on-chain operation. For most wallets, this is opening a new channel. However, the Phoenix wallet for example only has one channel and can use a technology called splice-in to make it larger.

*Image: splice-in. New resources come into the channel, making the original channel larger. A splice-in is a single on-chain transaction that merges Bitcoins from the original channel, adds funds from the new channel, resulting in a larger channel. Source: Phoenix wallet.*

How to approach capacity? If you can manage to pay the occasional on-chain fee, then with regular non-custodial end-user wallets you don't have to deal with capacity. If it's not enough, the wallet provider will increase it for you. This is true with wallets like Breez or Phoenix, for example.

If we use Lightning more often and are sensitive to fees, it's important to understand the capacity and maybe plan a bit. A typical example of when we should look at fees is especially in cases where we want to accept (receive) payments more frequently and we rarely send. This can be for example if we want to accept Bitcoins via Lightning in our business, or if we plan to use Lightning to purchase Bitcoins using a Dollar cost averaging (DCA) strategy.

Why don't we need to be so interested in sending? If we look back at the bucket analogy, the water we want to pour into someone else's bucket is already in the bucket, so we never need a new bucket to send via Lightning - the water is already in a bucket.

The question is how do we get the incoming liquidity - if we use a wallet such as Phoenix wallet, we get it from the liquidity provider. In the case of Phoenix, it's directly the authors of the wallet - if there is insufficient capacity, the operator in cooperation with your wallet will open a new channel, move the old channel's funds to it and the payment will go through. In this case you have to pay an on-chain fee for the incoming payment.

If we know that we will receive more payments (e.g. from clients), we can buy incoming liquidity or otherwise create larger channel. It used to be that virtually the only way to do this was for someone to send us sats via Lightning (say, in the amount of 1M satoshi), we sent them back a little less, and we had a channel with incoming liquidity. Such an operation cost the sender some Lightning fee (0.4% if the sender is Phoenix) and us 0.4%, so the cost of this operation was about 0.8% + on-chain fee. Phoenix specifically allows you to buy incoming liquidity without anyone else to do this with. Although the fee is a bit higher (1%), Phoenix seems to guarantee the incoming liquidity for at least a year.

*Picture: water in the bucket are our sats in the channel (our balance). We can receive the channel capacity (bucket capacity) minus our balance. If we want to accept more, we need a new channel - a bigger bucket. Exchanging buckets is an on-chain transaction.*

Thus, if we regularly buy Bitcoins or accept payments, we can get liquidity equal to our estimated income for the next few months at once and pay one on-chain fee for a "big bucket". After that, the next transaction is free to receive.

For other wallets, this liquidity can be obtained in other ways - using the liquidity provider's service, or for other wallets we can even open channels manually.

The [Lightning Network+](#) service (lightningnetwork.plus) can help us to do this. It is a non-commercial service that allows us to exchange liquidity. The most common way is to join a so-called triangle where three sides (A, B and C) open channels between each other. A opens a channel with B, B opens a channel with C and C opens a channel with A. Thus, all three pay one on-chain fee each and each gets a channel with both outgoing and incoming liquidity. There are no other fees associated with this service, but it's a good idea to look at the terms and conditions - how long you have to leave the channel open, how many other channels you must already have, and in what capacity. This is usually not how you can open your first channel - but it's a good idea to open it with people in your community or on services you plan to interact with.

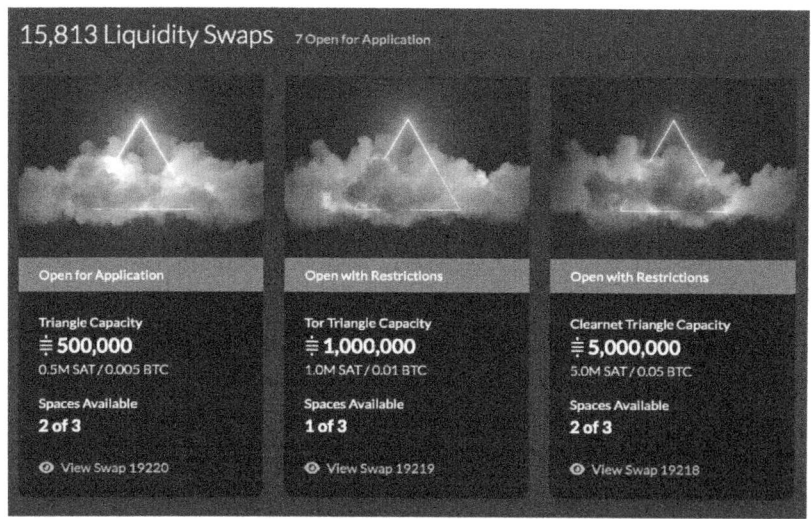

Image: the Lightning Network+ service that allows people to agree to create channels to share capacity. For example, the middle offer on the image is for a channel of a million satoshi in a "triangle", with one space free in this swap. If you want to join that triangle, you can open a channel and you get a channel with a million satoshi capacity to receive in return.

We'll stay with capacity - it's good to open channels when fees are lower. The maximum fee you are willing to pay is set by you if you open the channel directly, or you can find it in your wallet settings. It is possible that due to this setting you will not be able to accept payment when there is insufficient capacity, because the wallet needs to increase it and the wallet will not open the new channel due to the fees. Therefore, it is a good idea to schedule and open channels at times of lower fees - often this is at the weekend, for example. Or follow bitcoiners on X or on Nostr, they will often send a "good time to open Lightning channels" message.

## Security

Your Lightning wallet is only as secure as your device. Since every payment (sent, received, or just passing through) requires a signed transaction, all private keys are online on the computer (or a smartphone). We cannot manually sign transactions by confirming on a hardware wallet as with regular bitcoin payments. Thus, at least at the time of this writing, no one has yet created a hardware wallet for Lightning, although technically it is possible (similar to the Trezor Suite, where you can let a coinjoin run without having to confirm every single round).

With Lightning on a smartphone, I recommend to only have money for everyday spending and be careful about the security of your device.

How much is "for everyday spending" depends on each user. Breez wallet, for example, has a maximum wallet balance limit of 4 million satoshi. At that amount, they already recommend sending satoshi to a hardware wallet.

## How to back up Lightning

As the channel state changes, the backup of the Bitcoin wallet is not just a mnemonic seed (the familiar 12 or 24 words). For each channel, one needs to have the last backed up state (called a commit transaction), the revocation keys of all previous states, and other information. Since if you send an old state to the Bitcoin blockchain, you lose all the money in the channel, it is very important to have a current backup - a one second too old backup can mean you lose money because a payment flashed through you, although this is not an issue with mobile wallets, as they usually don't route payments for others.

What some wallets (like Phoenix) do is send backups to the cloud and encrypt them with a seed-derived key. In that case, the "backup" you see is just the seed, but it's good to know that you also need the operator's "cloud" service on the other side to work in order to restore it. It's unlikely that you'll need to restore your wallet while the other side doesn't operate anymore, but it's good to know about this problem - purely with the seed, you only get to access funds from fully closed channels.

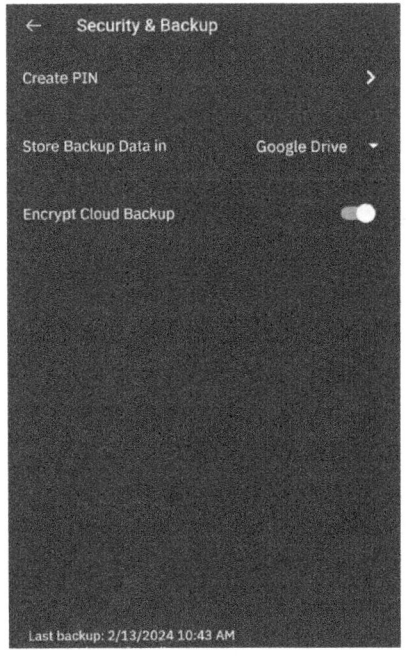

*Image: Breez wallet allows you to back up to the "cloud". The Android version allows backup to your own remote server or Google Drive, the iOS version also allows backup to Apple's iCloud. The backup is a standard backup, which can also be imported to the Lightning node called lnd, so it is completely independent of the existence of the Breez wallet. It's also encrypted, so you won't lose money in the event of a data leak from the cloud.*

Channel backup is not unified - each wallet has a different mechanism for this. There is a special type of backup, called static channel backup, which is usable in case of a major failure and no other current backup. This type of backup does not contain the last states, only which channels we have opened and with whom. Based on this static channel backup, we have the ability to ask the other party to close a channel - we don't have everything we need to do this ourselves, but at least we know who we can use the Lightning protocol to ask to close and which channels are involved. However, the other side may not comply, may not even be online, so it's not a 100% backup. On the other hand, we can use it when we're not sure if we have a current backup - or know we don't.

Incidentally, such a request to close a channel might encourage the counterparty to close a channel with an old state in which it is entitled to a larger balance. There are watchtowers to prevent it from doing so, which store the revocation keys of the old states and can punish the counterparty even if we do not have a backup of revocation keys. We do not have to trust these watchtowers, they have no way to misuse the information, they only know how to punish the counterparty in case it wants to commit fraud.

# Myths and differences between Lightning and Bitcoin on-chain

We will now introduce the Lightning network based on the myths and differences from the Bitcoin network.

## Are Lightning Bitcoins real Bitcoins?

This myth, or misunderstanding is quite common and comes from comparing the Lightning network to technologies such as sidechains (Liquid, Rootstock) or to various ways of "wrapping" bitcoins in other networks (WBTC, BTC.b). Let's now think about what Bitcoin is mainly in terms of ownership. Bitcoins are "stored" in a public database of balances where the network agrees on what addresses hold what amount.

I mentioned the traditional Bitcoiner saying - "not your keys, not your Bitcoin". This is partially true, but not all Bitcoins are actually protected by private keys, and it is not always necessary to have all private keys. In "classic" on-chain wallets, however, this is true - if you have private keys, you are able to create and sign a valid transaction that sends Bitcoins to another address.

In Lightning, you always have a valid transaction where you can take the balance due to you. You don't need anyone else's cooperation to do this - when you decide to send money, you can do it yourself, keeping sovereignty over your Bitcoin.

The only restriction is that you can only get your money to your address without working with a third party after the time lock expires, which ensures the counterparty can penalize broadcasting of the old transactions (old channel states). If you don't want to cooperate with anyone, you get your coins without any other party, you just take the last commit transaction (channel state) and send it to the Bitcoin network to be mined, and then after the time lock expires, take the money by signing the transaction with the key you have.

Of course, this isn't the most efficient way to get Bitcoins - the ideal is to not close the channel and just swap (for example, using the Boltz service mentioned above or your wallet's built-in functionality). Even if you want to close a channel, it's much better to do it with a counterparty with whom you have that channel open (cooperative close), as you don't have to wait and do another transaction, you can simply agree to close the channel and both sides side the closing transaction.

Image: Not every Bitcoin is the same. Image is from my book *Cryptocurrencies - Hack Your Way to a Better Life*. Sidechains are "bankcoins", because of counterparty risk, but Lightning is the real Bitcoin.

However, if we're addressing the question of whether it's "your bitcoins" or just a promise by someone else to redeem them on demand (which is the case with, say, the sidechains or other forms of bankcoin such as exchange balances). With Lightning you don't need anyone else to send the transaction, at worst, you just need to wait some time.

## Lightning has no addresses

Lightning network has no addresses. We make payment by creating a payment path to the node and paying the Lightning invoice. As such, the Lightning invoice is discarded after the payment goes through and we don't need to store it anywhere – nor it would work again. Lightning has quite a bit more privacy than on-chain payments, and there is no publicly available permanent record of individual payments (unlike the Bitcoin blockchain) - a payment made just changes the distribution of payment channel balances. Your wallet can of course remember what it has paid and what it has received, but this is only for accounting purposes and to show history.

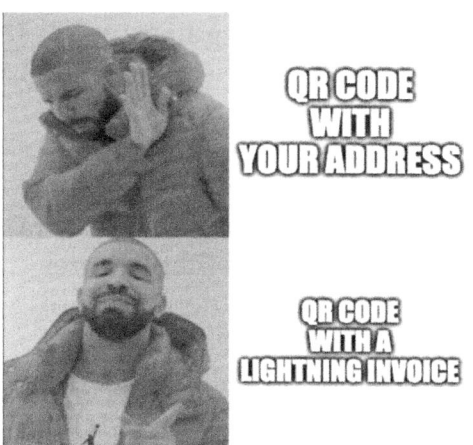

*Image: Lightning invoices work a little differently than Bitcoin addresses. Ask for a lightning invoice, not an address.*

Since the cooperation of both parties (and the part of the Lightning network we use as a payment path) is required to pay a Lightning invoice, the invoice contains information on how to contact the other party, what public key we can use, what payment (what amount) is involved, a description of the payment, and the expiration date. After the expiration date, the invoice can no longer be paid and a new one needs to be created. This is convenient because of Bitcoin exchange rate changes - the amount in Bitcoin is often only valid for a limited time, but a Bitcoin payment request, for example, can be paid at any time.

New developments bring something like addresses to Lightning. First, there is a Lightning address standard, which looks like an e-mail address. This standard relies on the DNS infrastructure and is often provided by custodial providers. This is also how zaps work on Nostr (a censorship-resistant social network that features tight integration with the lightning network).

Second – there is a new standard called BOLT12, which allows for reusable payment requests, that can be used similarly to addresses. On the background, they are just a way to negotiate a one-time invoice. You can't for example see how much has been sent to this QR code.

## Lightning has no history

Unlike on-chain payments, Bitcoins sent via Lightning have no history. The payment will come by an accounting change (an on-chain transaction enforceable on chain if needed) through the payment channel you have open. Thus, the Bitcoins that the sender sends are in no way related to what coins you receive. For this reason, it's a good idea to use Lightning when accepting Bitcoins, because you don't have to deal with whether the coins in question are on some list of dirty coins, whatever one's opinion of those lists may be.

# Finality - transactions are confirmed immediately

If we have an open channel through which we receive, we don't have to wait for payment confirmation by miners. After the payment is confirmed by our wallet, we have the coins and the transaction is final.

Image: Anyone who has been trying to buy sats from someone and froze in a dark underpass in gloves, scarf and hat will appreciate that with Lightning there is no need to wait for confirmations from miners and transactions are final instantly. Go P2P, trade!

Even if the channel needs to be enlarged due to insufficient receiving capacity, there is no need to wait because the sender cannot do a double-spend. The risk of non-confirmation of the transaction in this case is only between the receiver and their channel partner, so if you believe that the wallet operator does not want to cheat you, there is no point in freezing out in the cold and waiting for confirmation.

## Fees

Lightning fees are not free. Liquidity is locked in the channel and to unlock it you need to make an on-chain transaction in the worst-case scenario. Therefore, individual players in the lightning network charge fees for forwarding payments. These depend on the amount, not size of the transaction, as would be the case with on-chain transactions.

The fees are usually lower and for small amounts (such as Nostr zaps) they are cheaper than on-chain fees. At the same time, the fees are very independent of how full the Bitcoin blocks are. Therefore, it is good to open channels at times of lower fees, and it is possible to send cheap payments through the open channel then. However, for larger amounts it may already be worthwhile to make an on-chain payment.

| TRANSACTION FEES | | | |
|---|---|---|---|
| No Priority | Low Priority | Medium Priority | High Priority |
| 10 sat/vB | 27 sat/vB | 29 sat/vB | 30 sat/vB |
| $0.73 | $1.96 | $2.10 | $2.18 |

*Figure: Whether Lightning fees or on-chain fees are more worthwhile depends mainly on on-chain fees, as fees on the Lightning network are much more stable. A good source for the current status of on-chain fees can be found, for example, [at mempool.space](at mempool.space).*

How high are the fees? I did a comparison on my blog (Test of Bitcoin Lightning wallets), but it's already a bit out of date. The heuristic is that the fee is usually around 0.4% of the amount sent at most (the recipient pays nothing for receiving through an existing channel with sufficient capacity). At the time I am writing these lines, the fee for including a normal transaction with two inputs and two outputs in the next block is about 2240 sats, so for an amount above 560k sats, an on-chain payment may already be worthwhile. But do your own calculation, the fees are changing all the time and might be much higher.

# Lightning Ecosystem

The Lightning network has quite a rich ecosystem of projects and companies. Most of us think of wallets as the first category, but those are only a small part of the whole ecosystem. Since channel capacity is key, there is a new category of providers: liquidity service providers, or channel capacity providers.

Of course, we also have providers of various services via Lightning, the social network Nostr, e-cash systems, exchanges that allow deposits and withdrawals via Lightning, payment gateways that help you with acceptance, [podcasting 2.0 applications](), and voucher services.

Services are being created at the speed of light(-ning). Therefore, any recommendations on specific wallets and services may be obsolete before the ink on this article dries.

# Wallets

With the Lightning ecosystem, we will be primarily interested in wallets, as that is the first thing users will encounter when using Lightning. The wallet ecosystem is varied - from the Lightning nodes that an experienced system administrator installs on their server (lnd, core lightning, eclair, phoenixd, ...), to distributions that provide other services besides the node itself (e.g. btcpayserver or btcpayserver-docker, Cryptoanarchistic Debian Repository, or the more DIY umbrel, citadel, RaspiBlitz, myNode, StartOS, nodl, ...).

*Image: Home nodes will provide Lightning and Bitcoin nodes for ourselves, our families and our communities, in addition to data storage, e-cash mint, or other services. If you want to be your own bank, it's a good idea to have a simple home server that allows you to be in control of your data. Source: [Cypherpunk visions and trends 2023-2025](#).*

Of course, the wallet (including the lightning node) can also be run on a mobile device, or a home laptop or desktop computer. Wallets differ in what they provide and what control they give the user.

We will not consider Custodial wallets - they are not Bitcoin (or Lightning) wallets, they provide access to third-party banking services, and thus go against the essence of Bitcoin itself.

Easy to use, the second-generation Lightning wallets help users with liquidity and possible swap operations. Probably the most well-known wallets are [Phoenix](Phoenix) and [Breez](Breez). Both run on iOS and Android, but they take different approaches. Breez runs a full lnd node, which on mobile does direct payment routing.

In addition, it integrates with, for example, podcast playback and other services. It also provides liquidity and swap-in or swap-out services to receive and send on-chain payments. By providing routing, the wallet tends to be slower and needs to synchronize more with the network - both with the Bitcoin blockchain (to see if someone has closed the channel) and with the peer to peer lightning network (to keep track of nodes and to route payments securely). This is a rather interesting concept, where the authors are trying to experiment with the new possibilities that Lightning offers. That's also why they have a limitation to a maximum balance of 4M satoshi.

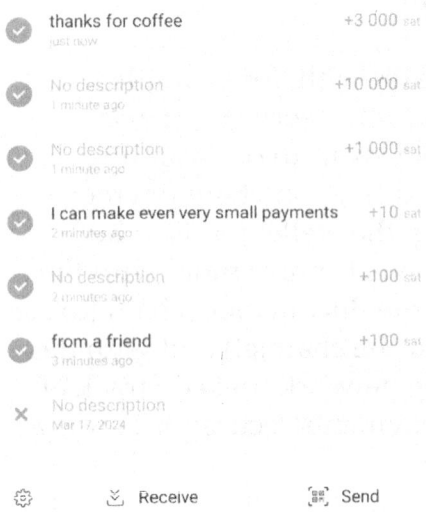

*Image: the Phoenix wallet is one of the simple wallets. You basically need two buttons to operate it: Receive and Send.*

In contrast, Phoenix brings simplicity, less data intensity and predictability, at the expense of some privacy and the lack of diversity of services provided. Payments are routed by the operator's server - so the user has a lightning node, but the lightning node delegates tasks such as creating a payment path to the server. Phoenix, on the other hand, unlike Breez, supports connectivity over the Tor anonymization network directly.

Even though Phoenix delegates many tasks to the server, the private keys are still controlled by the user's app on the phone, so it is not a custodial wallet. Phoenix has a simple fee structure (0.4% per payment sent, on-chain fee per payment received). The downside is also low on-chain privacy, as the same address is still used to receive on-chain payments, and the funds are connected to an existing channel using splice-in (but you can use an external service like boltz.exchange to solve this problem).

*If you want to see a video demonstration of how to install and use Phoenix Wallet, check my free (no sign-up required) course "A quick introduction to Bitcoin – wallet setup, buying, payments[1]". which is available for free and without registration. In it, you'll find other tutorials on how to use Bitcoin, how to buy Bitcoins in a vending machine, or how to use the Vexl app to find a counterparty to buy from or sell bitcoin to.*

---

[1] https://hackyourself.io/bitcoin-intro

Both Phoenix and Breez have one Bitcoin balance - unlike other wallets, you don't have an "on-chain" and a "lightning" balance, but all your satoshi are in a Lightning channel, from which you can also send them to an on-chain address. Other wallets (Mutiny, Zeus, etc) separately show Lightning and on-chain balances and allow you to convert between them. With these wallets, you have more control, but also more things to understand and handle yourself.

Another type of wallet is web (Progressive Web Apps) wallets. A good representative of such a wallet is the Mutiny Wallet, which'll cover later in the book . This wallet bypasses the censorship of the App Store and Google Play and thus can afford to experiment with other tools.

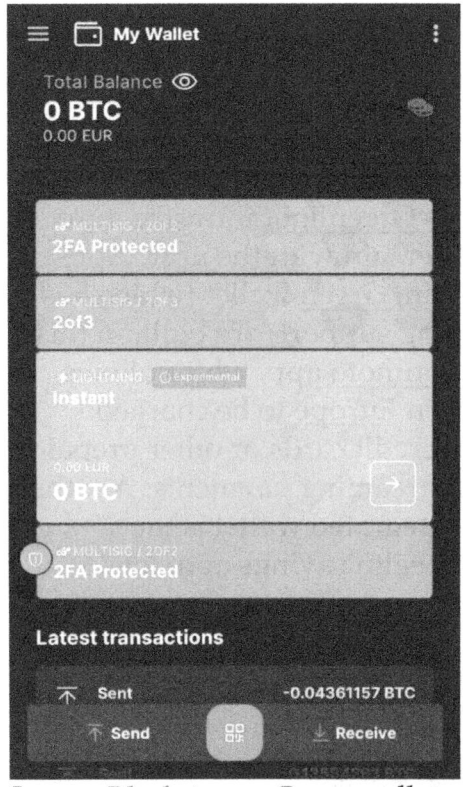

Image: Blockstream Green wallet with experimental Lightning support, which also supports separate on-chain balances and the Liquid network. It also supports multisig-protected accounts.

The authors of the Breez wallet, in collaboration with Blockstream, have also created the Breez SDK - a tool you can use to integrate Lightning into your app. This is a model somewhat similar to Phoenix, where some of the functionality is taken over by Blockstream's Greenlight infrastructure, but the private keys remain with the user. Apps such as the Blockstream Green wallet (which has experimental Lightning support) are built on this SDK, as well as the Satimoto app, which allows electric cars in Western Europe to be charged without the need for credit cards or other prepaid cards - purely using streaming payments. Another innovation with an integrated wallet is the Crowdhealth group health savings app, for example.

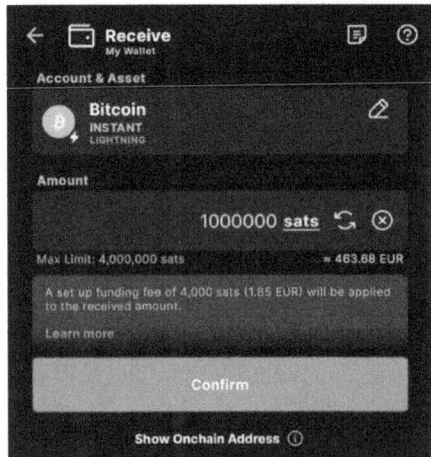

*Image: when you receive via Blockstream Green, you can see the charges that are charged for opening the channel (capacity increase) after paying a given lightning invoice. The fees are very similar from service to service.*

Some wallets allow you to get even more control, for example Blixt Wallet or Zeus does allow you to open channels automatically, but you can also open channels manually or buy liquidity from multiple providers. So, unlike Phoenix and Breez, you are not limited to channels with a wallet provider, but you can choose who you want to keep a channel open with. Beware, however, that channels with mobile wallets are closed by many nodes, as the channel is often unusable for routing and is therefore frozen liquidity that node operators can use elsewhere. So don't be surprised if such a randomly opened channel is closed by the counterparty after a while - if you want stable liquidity, you often need to buy it or use your own node.

You can use your own node with Zeus wallet. It will allow you to connect to your core lightning or lnd node or to a node that supports the lndhub protocol (such as lnbits). That means that you can use a wallet on your mobile that securely communicates with your home node. However, Zeus allows you to run the node on your device as well. It can open channels automatically using the built-in Olympus liquidity provider, but you can also interact with other liquidity providers and you can also open your own channels.

There's another type of wallets that are "kind-of-Lightning". Muun and Aqua are worth mentioning. The Muun wallet pretends to be a Lightning wallet, but has a unified on-chain balance and converts every Lightning payment (both incoming and outgoing) into an on-chain payment using a so called "submarine swaps". The problem is that you pay on-chain fees with every transaction. This is proving to be a not-so-good idea in a high-fee environment.

Image: the Aqua Wallet allows you to use the Liquid network and integrates the swap service between Liquid and Lightning into the user interface. This means that you can scan the QR code of a Lightning invoice (or paste it) and pay it without having any channel open. Blocks on the Liquid network take exactly one minute to create, so even if the network is waiting for a confirmation, it will average 30 seconds. However, the trial payment went through almost instantly and at 10,000 sats the total charge was 426 sats, which is still quite a high charge at such low amount, but there may be an advantage in not having to deal with capacity when accepting larger payments.

The Aqua wallet works similarly but does on-chain transactions on the Liquid network, which has lower fees. You don't have to worry about liquidity, channel capacity, etc. However, the swap doesn't always work reliably, but that might be because this wallet is still relatively new to the market (especially its Lightning support).

## Accepting Lightning payments at premises

You can use any wallet with sufficient channel capacity or suitable conditions to accept Lightning payments. It is possible to use a Phoenix wallet (ideal when purchasing liquidity).

https://hackyourself.io/breez-pos
Video: Demonstration of the Point of Sale mode of the Breez wallet - easy acceptance of Bitcoins using Lightning in your establishment

The Breez and Zeus wallets have a dedicated "Point of Sale" mode, designed expressly for accepting payments in establishments. You can create products or protect the sending of Bitcoins from the wallet with an additional "admin" password, protecting your wallet balance from device theft.

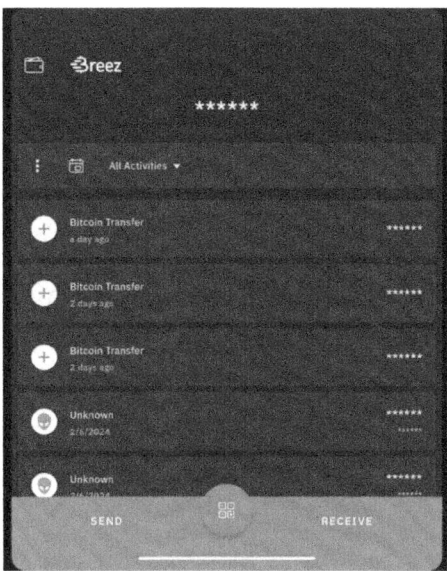

*Image: the Breez wallet (but also, for example, the Phoenix wallet) allows you to hide balances and amounts. That means you can open the wallet in the presence of someone else (a customer, or an OTC trader) without showing them your current balance.*

Of course, you can also use the PoS module of btcpayserver to accept payments, but you need to run a full Lightning node on the server for that. For most users (small businesses, freelancers) a mobile app is sufficient.

# Usability and usage of lightning network

The other fundamental question is - who is using Lightning? A significant increase in the number of users is reported by all payment gateways and wallet authors.

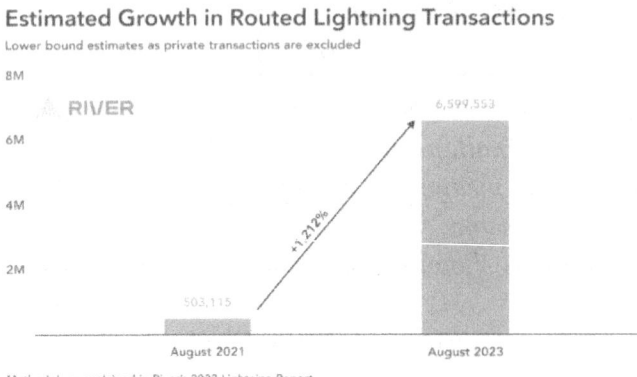

*Figure: Increase in the number of payments. This is a sophisticated estimate because many payments are simply not visible and we have no way of accounting for them. One reason for the increase is Nostr zaps. Source: River's 2023 Lightning Report.*

This is due to several factors. First, it is the quality of wallets, which recently have much fewer failed payments, are more user-friendly and so on. Add to that the increase in the number of Bitcoin users and the rise in on-chain fees. And also, the decline in popularity of altcoins, whose core value-add was lower fees.

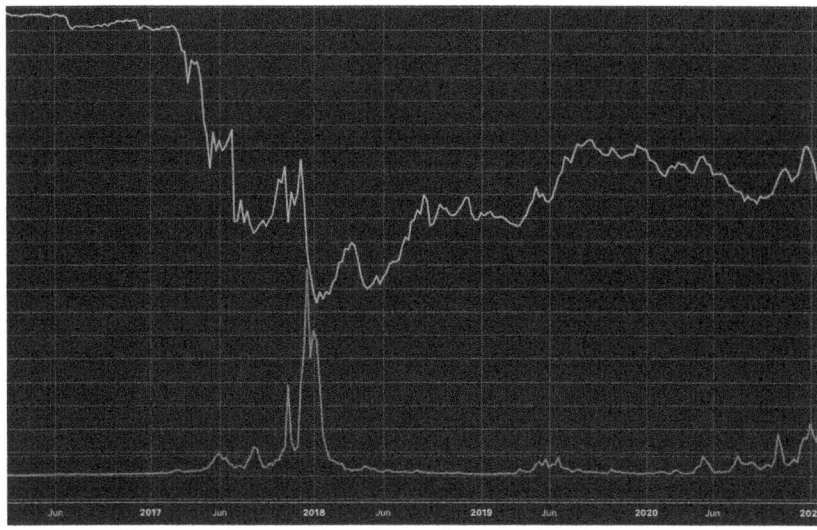

*Figure: The top line on the chart shows Bitcoin's percentage dominance over altcoins by market capitalization. The bottom one shows the average transaction fee in USD. We can see that in late 2017 and in 2021 when fees rose, market capitalization left Bitcoin for altcoins, but we don't see a significant drop in the last fee increase in late 2023 - more of a small increase. Is this due to the popularity of the Lightning network, which partially solves the fee problem? ETF approval or anything else could also be "to blame"... Source: <u>TradingView chart</u>*

Usage also increased by services that operate on the Lightning network and it is the only way of financial communication if you are using these services. This is for example the use of podcasting 2.0 services, where sats are streamed for every minute listened to, or the social network Nostr, where authors of posts can be rewarded with "zaps" (Lightning micropayments).

*Figure: The total number of Lightning micropayments (zaps) on the Nostr network over the last half year has reached more than 2.5 million. Source: stats.nostr.band*

# Lightning and privacy

On the Bitcoin blockchain, we only see channels opening and closing. Thus, the initial state and the ending state (split) of the channel between the counterparties. Looking at the transaction that opens the channel (the funding transaction), we can currently see that it is a 2-of-2 multisig address, but when we switch to taproot addresses in Lightning, this information is also lost and the transaction will look like any other transaction to a regular taproot address.

Closing a channel takes two forms - a cooperative close is one where both parties decide to close the channel and sign a transaction with the last state and send it to the network. A cooperative channel close looks like a transaction with one multisig input and two outputs (the amount attributable to Alice and the amount attributable to Bob), so from the network's point of view it is a fairly standard transaction (in the case of a taproot, it won't even be visible that it is a multisig).

Non-cooperative channel closure (e.g., when the counterparty is off-line for an extended period of time) is worse off from a privacy perspective; if we look at the entire channel closure sequence, it is clear that it is a Lightning channel closure.

But what's important - the channel is with a specific counterparty and says nothing about who we sent the money to, it's just the end state of the distribution of funds in a particular channel. We don't see how many payments came in, went out, much less where.

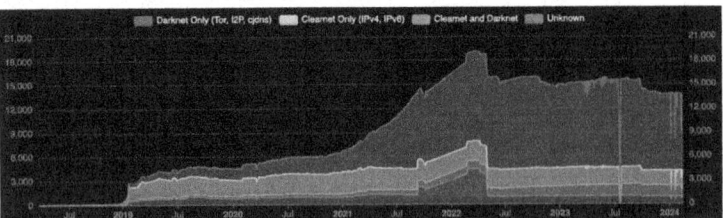

Figure: Most nodes connect over the "darknet" (Tor, I2P or cjdns). This hides its IP address from the rest of the network. Source: mempool.space

However, with privacy, we also need to be mindful of other things - network privacy (IP addresses), identifiers on the network (public keys of individual nodes), and the actual communication in the Lightning peer to peer network.

We can protect IP addresses with a VPN or Tor. In addition, communication does not have to take place directly, but through other nodes on the network. The identifier in the network is mainly the identifier of the recipient. This is currently more or less permanent, but if you care about it, you can also use temporary keys, for example using the lnproxy project.

The question is whether any attacker can see the payments. The answer is very hardly, and even then, only if they are directly looking at the network at the moment the payment goes through. After the payment has been made, all that is left of it is a signed invoice with a pre-hash (that is, a confirmation that the payment has been made), which is available to the sender. If he does not show it to anyone, there is no permanent public record of the payment. If the receiver does not want such a receipt to exist, he can use lnproxy to create an invoice with a temporary key that is not linked to him.

Individual nodes do not see all the traffic - the sender creates the path itself, by communicating with the nodes. They don't even know if they are just forwarding the payment for someone else or communicating with the sender.

Individual nodes do not even know whether they are sending the whole amount, only a part of it, or even more than the amount being sent. How is this possible? A single payment can go through multiple nodes, so if we are paying someone a million satoshi, the path can be made up of different branches with smaller amounts.

*Figure: A payment path through multiple channels that branch off. If a node sees one leg of the payment path, it does not know if it is all the water from the river (the entire payment) or if it is just one leg, since communication with other nodes is encrypted - the other legs of the river are invisible to the node in one leg.*

Based on this, one could say that if a node along the payment path sees a payment, it knows that the payment is at least the amount it is forwarding - it doesn't know if the payment is more than the 100K satoshi it is forwarding, but it is unlikely to be less than that. However, this is also not the case, at least in theory. After all, the payment doesn't have to end up in one place - one can create a path that also rebalances the channels, and thus one of the recipients is the sender himself. He can send, say, a million satoshi, of which 1000 satoshi is the payment for a Nostr zap and the rest is forwarding money to himself through another channel, making his channels better rebalanced. Thus, a node that sees that it is forwarding 100 thousand satoshi from this path cannot assume that the payment is greater than or equal to 100 thousand satoshi, because it is in fact a payment of 1000 satoshi.

So Lightning privacy is good enough - on-chain payments are not easily visible, there is no publicly traceable permanent record of payments, coins have no history (so we don't have to deal with "dirty coins"), network privacy is provided by multiple layers (e.g. Tor), and moreover, any potential attacker has to make his attack exactly at the time of the payment, after the payment is completed, only the changed channel balances remain.

# On-chain privacy using Lightning

We can use the Lightning network to increase the privacy of on-chain transactions, sort of like a coinjoin replacement.

From a privacy perspective, an on-chain transaction vs. lightning is night and day. An on-chain transaction is transparent and visible to all, including source addresses (or outputs of other transactions) and amounts. There is no permanent record about lightning transactions.

## Accepting on-chain payments with privacy

Imagine you have two people you want to accept payment from. And then you want to pay for something in a shop.

Senders do not yet know how to make lightning payments and want to send money to an on-chain address (this can be an OTC trader for example, bitcoin ATM or an exchange, for example). Receiving into a Lightning wallet like Breez as two separate on-chain transactions (Breez: Receive via BTC address) will not directly link these transactions.

Practical example: we want to accept 0.01 BTC from person A and 0.015 BTC from person B. We can do this in the Breez wallet in sequence: we create one address to receive and send it to person A (careful, we can't send it to two people at once!). When he sends the transaction and it is extracted, we will have a balance in our Lightning wallet. Then we do the same procedure for user B. We now have a balance of 0.025 BTC in our wallet. What if we want to pay someone 0.02 BTC? The easiest way to do this is with a Lightning payment, but we can also do it by sending BTC to an on-chain address. In this case, since the swap towards the on-chain address is a third-party service (Boltz), we will never create a transaction in which we combine Bitcoins from user A and B. Thus, if our goal is to keep A from knowing that we are expecting 0.015 BTC from B, he will not know this from the chain analysis.

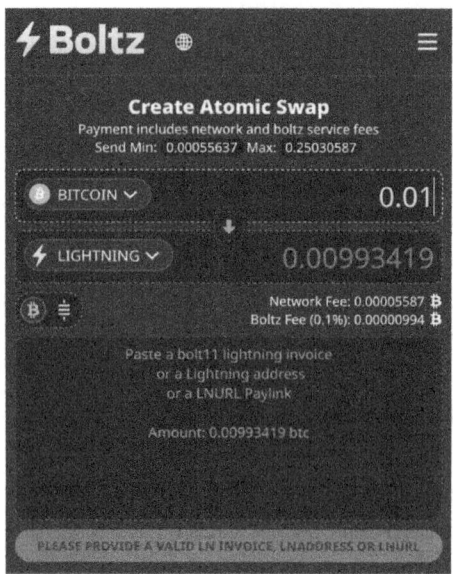

*Image: converting on-chain Bitcoins to Lightning payment using boltz.exchange.*

If you use a wallet other than Breez, it's important to look at how the payments look on-chain. For example, the current Phoenix wallet accepts all on-chain payments by swapping them into the single channel, so all on-chain payments are easily associated with the channel and with each other. However, that doesn't mean it's unsolvable - using boltz.exchange, you can convert on-chain Bitcoins into a lightning balance. In doing so, these payments/balances will not be outwardly linked, as the receiving Lightning wallet and the Boltz service are run by different entities.

Mind you, this doesn't mean that the link is necessarily untraceable - with enough court orders, I can imagine that services will be able to trace it from their logs over time (although they'll have a bit harder time with the Breez wallet, as the wallet itself also provides payment routing). The bottom line is that it doesn't create a publicly available permanent record. For people just observing the Lightning network and the Bitcoin blockchain, this is a very tough nut to crack.

## Watch out for correlations using amounts

The procedure of accepting 0.0142323 BTC via a swap from on-chain to Lightning and then supposedly "anonymously" sending 0.01416114 BTC out to another on-chain address in a few minutes is not a very secure way of anonymizing, because it is already clear at a glance that it is the same money (the second amount includes some swap fee and is therefore lower). Therefore, it is a good idea to wait for the incoming swaps to add up, or add money via Lightning and send out unrelated, higher amount. If I receive 0.0142323 BTC via on-chain and send 0.02 out because I had an additional balance in my Lightning wallet, it's harder to link.

## Lightning or coinjoin?

Personally, I prefer this method over mixing using coinjoins with Whirlpool or Wasabi because it's less conspicuous and less controversial. I use reputable services for Lightning->on-chain swap-outs, and I don't "swap" money with unknown people with questionable reputational risk. Such coins from reputable sources are also preferred by centralized institutions that evaluate the risk of each transaction (but it's best for them to accept Lightning payments and save the hassle of analyzing the chain – which they are often forced by regulations).

You get lost in the crowd, but not as a person who mixes coins, but as a person who uses a wallet in a standard way like thousands of other users of the same wallet.

Of course, it also depends on the amounts - if you have 1 BTC or more, you will encounter various Lightning capacity limits and channel opening fees.

# On-chain with Phoenix and Breez

Both Phoenix and Breez allow you to accept and send on-chain payments. However, they are quite different in this functionality. Phoenix does both sending and receiving using their splicing technology. This means that accepting an on-chain payment adds funds to the channel, i.e. it creates a transaction that uses funds from an existing channel, adds new on-chain funds you are receiving to them, and thus creates a new unified channel.

Sending an on-chain payment takes the on-chain transaction that the channel is funded with and withdraws the on-chain funds from there, sends the rest back and opens a new channel with the change.

This means that for on-chain payments, liquidity changes with Phoenix. Receiving an on-chain payment is two on-chain transactions - one is sending the funds to a swap-in on-chain address, and the other is used to add confirmed funds to the payment channel. Doing this second payment is still quite expensive, as it spends funds from a 2-of-2 multisig address. However, soon the channels will also switch to the taproot musig scheme, which will solve this problem.

Sending funds using Phoenix on-chain is one transaction, though also a bit more expensive, for the same reason.

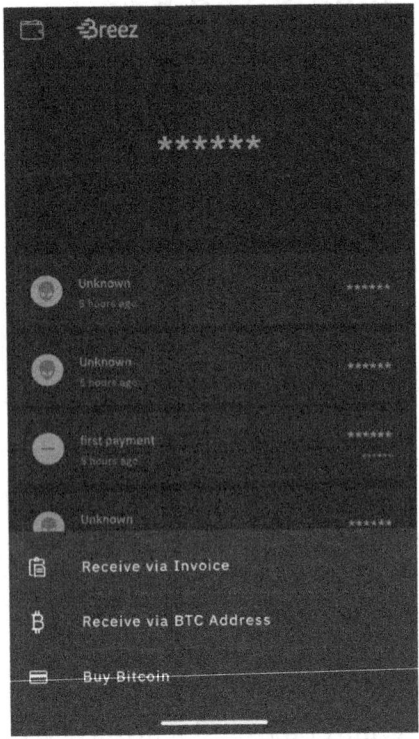

*Image: after pressing the Receive button in Breez, we have to choose how we want to receive Bitcoins. "Receive via Invoice" is to receive over the Lightning network (this is probably what we will use most often). "Receive via BTC Address" is receiving via on-chain payment. "Buy Bitcoin" is an integrated service for buying Bitcoins using fiat.*

Receiving on-chain to Breez Wallet is using their own service. After sending funds to the generated address (you get it via the Receive button and the "Receive via BTC Address" option), you will receive the exact amount you send without any fees if you already have a channel. If you do not have enough liquidity, the fee is 0.4% from the received amount. You will see this on the screen with the Bitcoin address.

The Bitcoin that you send to the swap-in address will have nothing to do with your channels - Breez collects them and opens new channels for users with them. They will be completely unrelated to your wallet, which is a nice privacy feature.

Sending on-chain from Breez works via Boltz.exchange, but it is integrated into the wallet. You don't lose liquidity, the Bitcoins sent are also not related to your coins, but Boltz requires a fee for this service. In addition, it's two on-chain transactions, which is important from a security perspective (you don't have to trust the Boltz service, it's an atomic swap), but such an on-chain send gets expensive. Worse yet, the recipient doesn't see the second transaction until the first transaction is confirmed. This makes sending Bitcoins to services such as payment gateways that require a transaction to be sent within some time practically unusable, since you cannot guarantee sending within some time (or you will significantly overpay in fees).

# Mutiny Wallet

The Mutiny Wallet is a non-custodial wallet for bitcoin (both on-chain and Lightning) that runs in the browser. This means that users have complete control over their own funds and are not subject to censorship by app stores such as Google Play and Apple's App Store. The wallet works without third party custody of your keys and **runs the Lightning node** directly in the browser locally via JavaScript and WASM technologies.

## Desktop version

Let's try the desktop version first. When you visit the Mutiny Wallet page, you'll be presented with a newly generated wallet that you can start using right away.

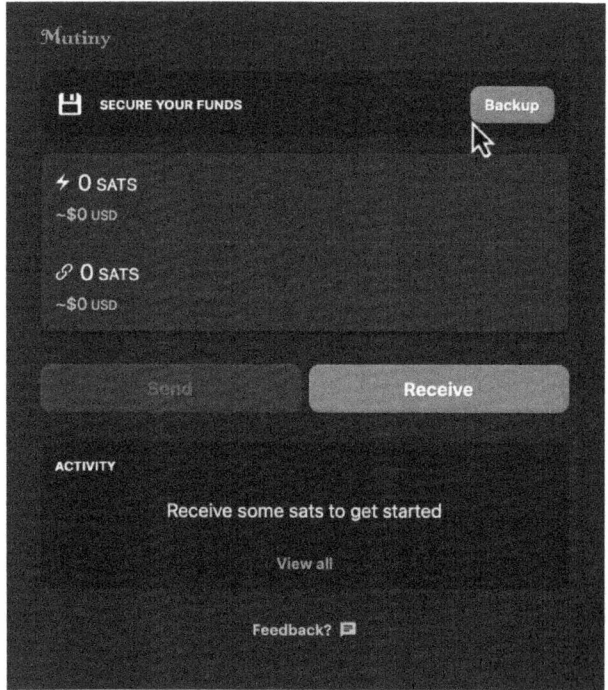

*Image: Mutiny Wallet automatically generates keys when opened and can be used immediately. There is no need to go into any menu and create a new wallet.*

At a glance, we can see that Mutiny does not (unlike e.g. Phoenix or Breez) have a unified balance - we have a separate balance for on-chain Bitcoin and Lightning Bitcoin.

The keys for both are automatically stored in your browser (local storage), but you can easily lose them there, so it's a good idea to click the Backup button and create a backup.

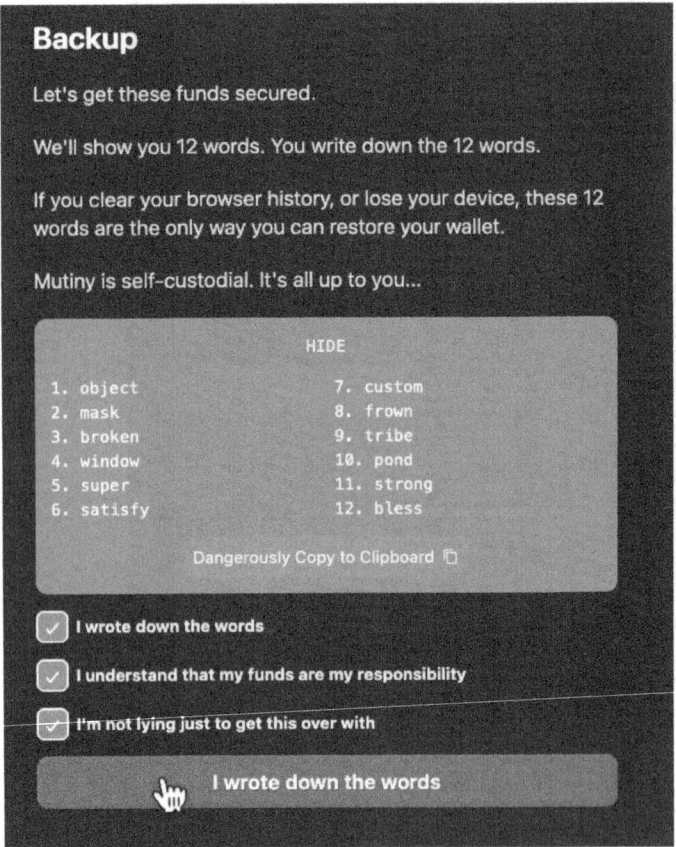

*Image: Seed backup. The last check mark "I am not lying just to get this over with" is nice, please respect it.*

Once we've made a backup, we can add an additional password to encrypt the keys in the browser - if someone gets to our device, they'll need this password to decrypt the seed. However, this is not the classic "passphrase" as we know it from other wallets.

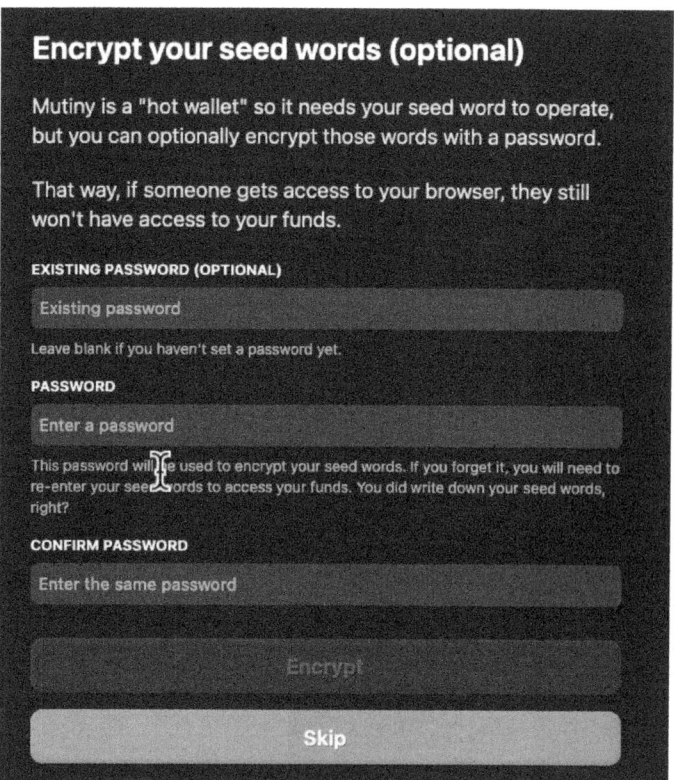

*Image: Optional password to encrypt the seed. If you are using Mutiny as a wallet for quick payments and don't have a lot of money in there, and while using the device yourself, and the device is sufficiently protected from unauthorized access, you can skip entering the password.*

In order to start using the wallet, we need to send some sats to it. I recommend starting directly through Lightning, you will get liquidity directly in the form of a channel. At the time of writing, the minimum amount of the first payment is 50,000 sats. From the incoming payment, 10,000 sats will be deducted as a fee for opening the channel and liquidity. The channel that will be opened towards you will be slightly larger than the amount you send, so you can receive further payments without opening a channel.

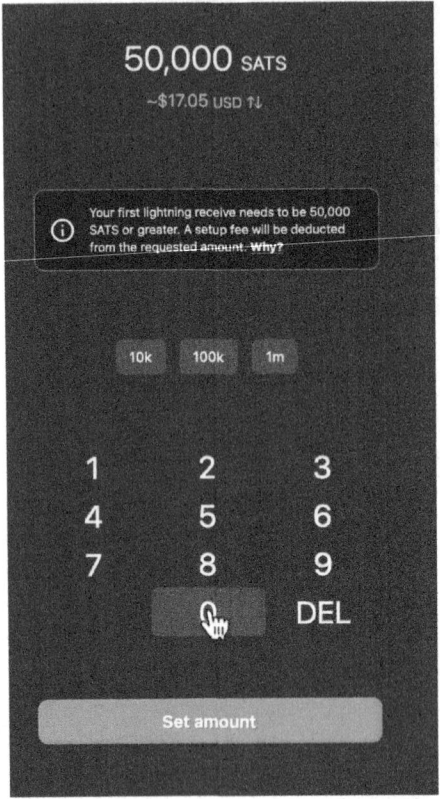

*Image: We receive a payment of 50,000 sats.*

I like that Mutiny will automatically show a unified QR code that contains both the Bitcoin on-chain address and the lightning invoice. You as a user don't have to choose what code you want to generate. If you send to this code with a Lightning wallet that supports unified codes, the payment is either transferred automatically via Lightning or you get to choose as a sender how you want to make the payment.

Image: Unified QR code for Bitcoin on-chain payment and Lightning invoice

If you have a wallet that doesn't know the unified codes yet, it's probably a good idea to think about switching to a different wallet, because it's a strong sign that someone doesn't care.

After payment, you will get a nice screen with the payment received and you will see the new balance:

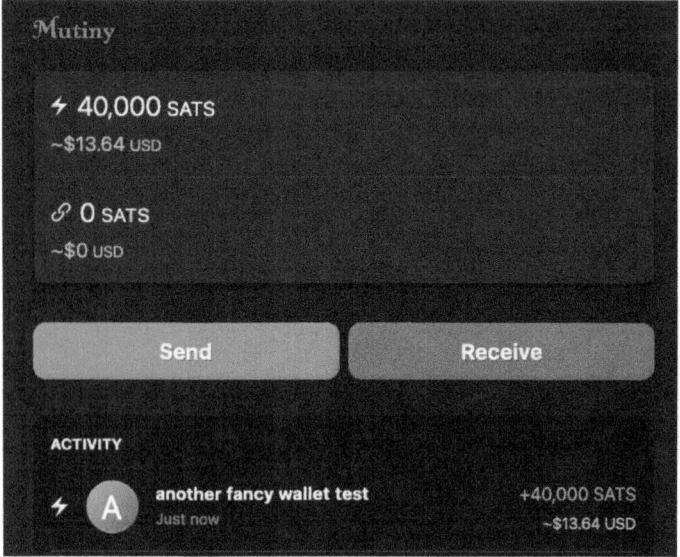

*Image: Wallet page after receiving the first payment. We can see the updated Lightning balance, the on-chain balance remained the same.*

Now let's try to send the payment. In the left menu we will find the send icon (paper airplane).

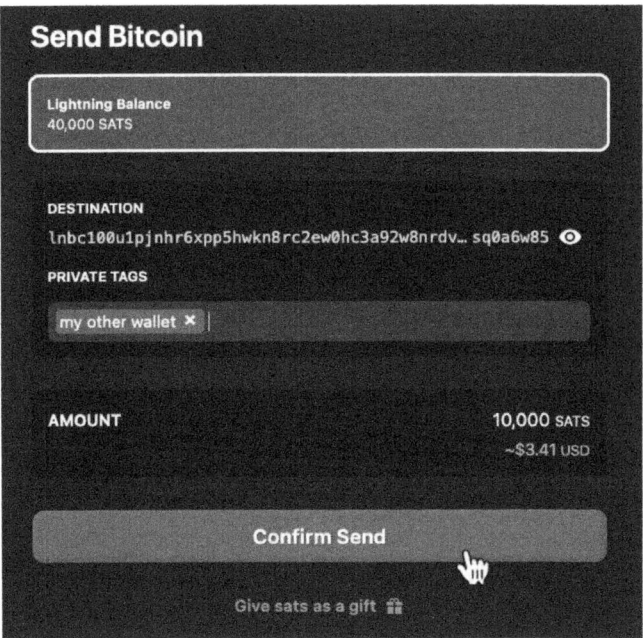

*Image: When sending, we choose where we want to send from (in this case we only have Lightning balance), where we want to send to and we can write the payment description that will be just for us to recognize this payment (this description is not sent to the counterparty).*

Many people with websites (or PWAs) wonder if the QR code scanning functionality works, if it is not a native app. It works, even on a desktop browser:

*Image: The QR code scanner works on both desktop and mobile devices. It even works with "continuity camera" on Apple devices, where you can use your mobile device as a camera instead of a desktop webcam. So, for example, you can sit at your laptop, make payments, but use your mobile device to scan QR codes.*

Let's look at the basic settings.

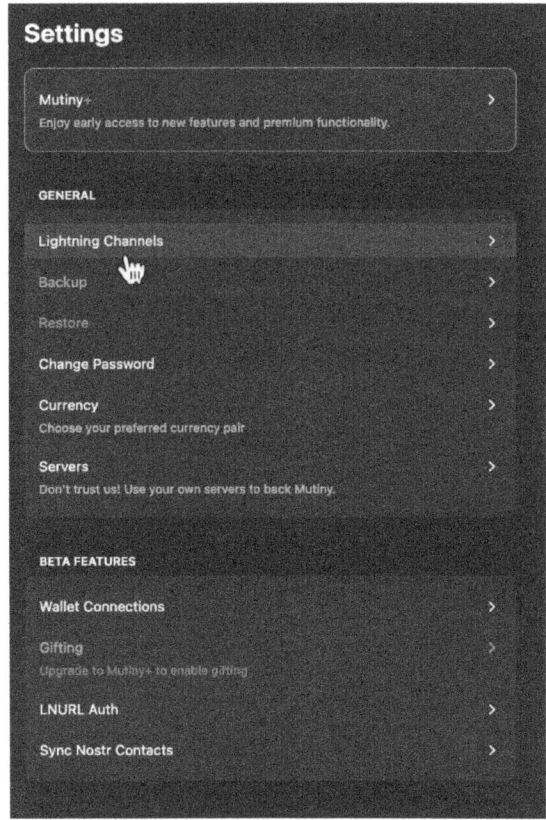

*Image: Settings - subscriptions, lightning feeds, backup and restore, change password, change fiat currency display, servers, LNURL login, etc.*

We mentioned that the liquidity provider used by Mutiny will add some liquidity to their side of the Lightning channel. We can see what kind of channels we have right in the settings under Lightning Channels.

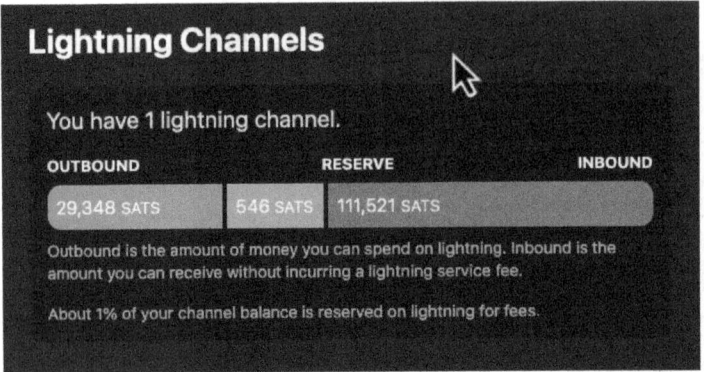

*Image: Lightning channel capacity - after payment we can send almost 30 thousand sats, we can receive a little over 110 thousand sats. This is despite the fact that the first payment was only 50 thousand sats. If we have multiple channels, this screen will show us all of them.*

In the fiat currency settings, we can choose the fiat currency in which to display the balance (except for satoshi, which is the main denomination).

The Mutiny wallet is open-source and thus it is possible to run it on your own server or your home node. In that case, you could also connect to it via the Tor Hidden Service, for example. To choose where the wallet connects to, there is a Servers tab where you can select the addresses of the individual services.

The front-end is a purely static site that directly contains the logic of the lightning node. Thus, the required servers wrap or make available some lightning or bitcoin network service - block explorer, liquidity provider, encrypted channel state store (encrypted with a key derived from your seed), etc.

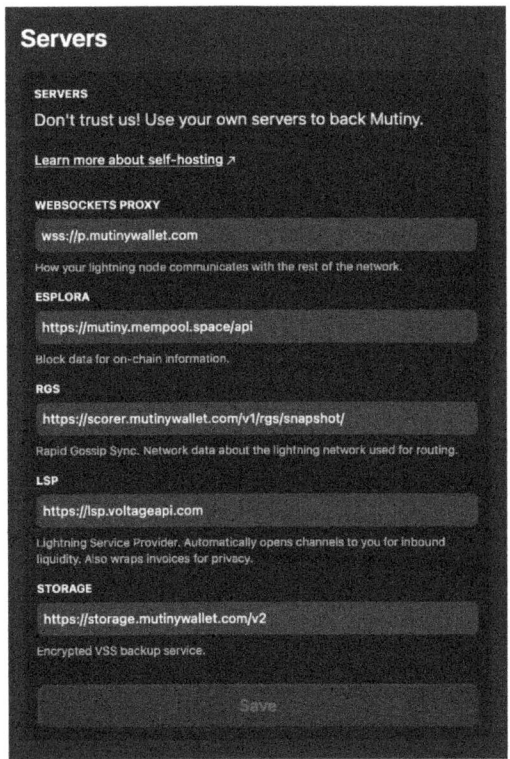

*Image: Server settings, especially important if you want to run the whole service yourself on your own infrastructure.*

# Mutiny on a mobile device as a Progressive Web App

If we open Mutiny Wallet on a new (mobile) device, we see an empty wallet, of course, because the wallet has created new keys. First, let's add it to our "Home Screen", which will make it a Progressive Web App - it will pretend to be like any other app on our device.

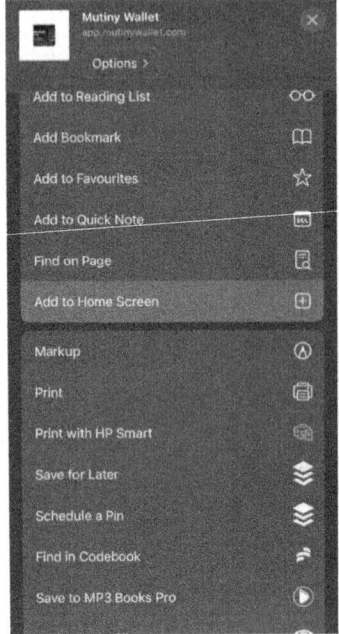

Image: On Apple devices, click the Share button and select "Add to Home Screen".

We will see a Mutiny Wallet icon, we can choose the description we want. By the way, if you want to use Mutiny as a Progressive Web App, I recommend to add it to the home screen first and then refresh it, because the PWA on the home screen will not remember the wallet otherwise.

Let's now restore the wallet backup.

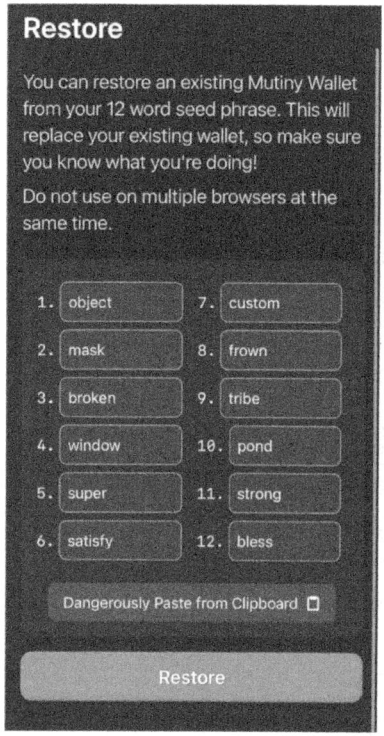

*Image: Restoring the wallet is easy, just enter the 12-word backup we created. Please don't use these words, it's not safe, I gave it to all the readers* ☺

If we do the restore shortly after closing Mutiny on the desktop, we get a window warning us that Mutiny is running somewhere else. This is so that the wallets don't fight each other over which is the main one. With on-chain wallets this wouldn't be a problem, but the Lightning wallet needs to have the most up-to-date state, or we may lose money. Mutiny is trying to play it safe here, and even a few minutes after closing a window with a wallet somewhere else, we still must wait a while.

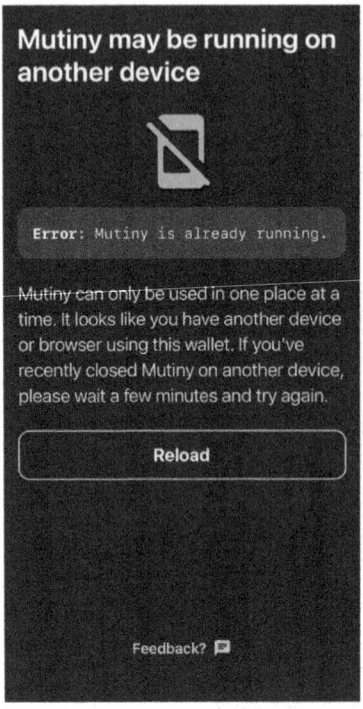

*Image: Warning that Mutiny is running elsewhere. We really need to wait a few minutes and then click reload to have the most up-to-date wallet state to complete the restore.*

If we move the wallet to another device in this way, it stops working on the original device - if we want to start using it on the original device, we must restore it again.

On a mobile device, the wallet then looks just like any other Lightning wallet - you won't even notice that it's just a sophisticated website.

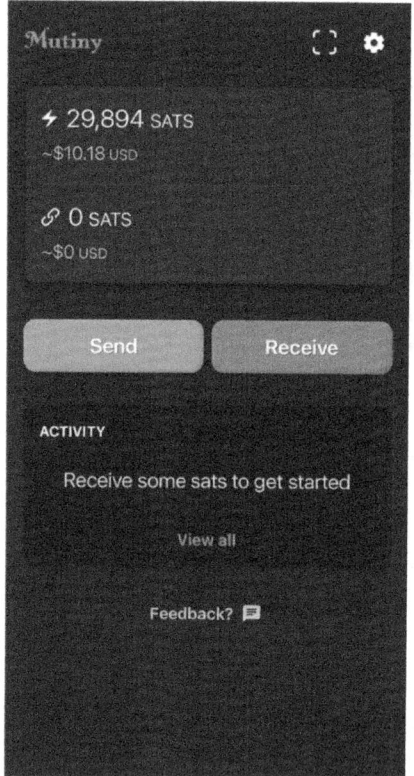

*Image: Mutiny wallet on a mobile device. We can see the restored balance from the other device.*

We can try a payment - we can use the Paste or Scan QR buttons and pay normally as if it were any other Lightning wallet.

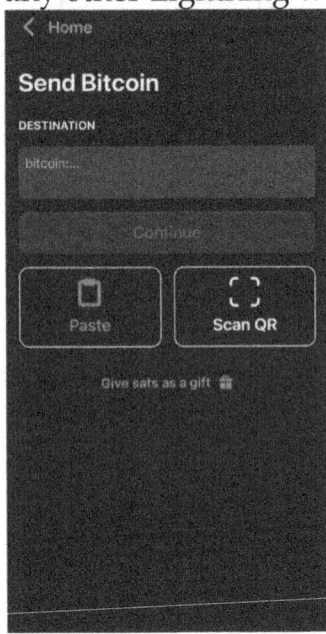

*Image: Sending Bitcoins supports scanning QR codes, even though it's a web app.*

Mutiny Wallet is a nice, modern wallet that you can use without even having to be logged into a store (App Store, Play Store, etc.).

It's good for very quickly onboarding users into Lightning without having to teach people about custodial wallets.

Personally, I'm often surprised at how many people have a smartphone that doesn't have any apps running. But every smartphone has a web browser.

## Progressive Web Application (PWA) and subscription option

As a Progressive Web App (PWA), Mutiny Wallet offers several advantages over traditional mobile apps. PWAs are installed on the user's device but are not downloaded from the app store. This means that they are not subject to the same restrictions as native apps, such as the need to go through an assessment (eligibility) process or the requirement to use an in-app purchase system.

Mutiny Wallet, for example, makes it possible for users to create subscriptions outside of the in-app purchase system (which Apple and Google take a cut of and, in the case of apps, have to go through them).

The first attempt to use this technology is the Mutiny+ subscription, which currently costs 16,000 sats per month (but this changes with the price of Bitcoin) and is paid for directly using Lightning. Regular subscription services have long been a problem with both Bitcoin and Lightning, and it's something Mutiny is experimenting with and wants to make this option available to other apps as well. Meanwhile, the app never just automatically takes the subscription, it still needs to be confirmed and the payment needs to be signed with private keys. But that doesn't mean the user can't indicate a willingness to subscribe to something and make the user interface work as seamlessly as possible.

However, the Progressive Web App form does have some drawbacks - first, you must trust the website operator not to have installed a backdoor. You might say to yourself that you must do that even with wallets from official stores - making a backdoor that the app store operator doesn't notice isn't such a problem after all. The difference, however, is that the app stores will produce evidence of the backdoor.

In addition, the update, or the same code, is applied to all users. However, the webserver may give different code to different users - so it may well be that the auditor sees the secure code without backdoor, and the user who has enough money there gets JavaScript that sends the money away without his knowledge. Of course, we have no reason to think that the operators of the official web version of Mutiny Wallet would do such a thing, but a web server hack is not entirely inconceivable. On the other hand, you can run your own front-end and back-end and use an "Uncle Jim" model. In recent versions you can even supplement this model with a home, family, or community Fedimint federation based on e-cash, that can be used in addition to on-chain and Lightning.

Another disadvantage of PWA is that it's harder to use in the background - for now, you really need to have the app open and waiting for an incoming payment. And of course you can't open links with the bitcoin: or lightning: URI scheme, so for payments you need to copy payment requests (invoices) and addresses - and then paste those into the Send bitcoin section. Alternatively, scan QR codes.

## Conclusion

Bitcoin has the advantage of diversity - it is similar to the web itself, or to email, or to operating systems derived from GNU/Linux. You can choose one of several ways to use it - you can zap users of Nostr from your Nostr client, use a number of mobile apps - custodial or self-custodial solutions, use e-cash systems, etc. The diversity is Bitcoin's strength. And Mutiny is a nice solution for those who don't want to tie themselves to platforms with app stores of big cellphone manufacturers.

Running a Lightning node directly in a web browser is not exactly a simple matter, so I see Mutiny as a bit of a test to see how far PWA technology can be taken. The vendors talk about big plans - in addition to subscription and making it available to third parties, they also want to implement value stabilization similar to the 10101 platform using Discreet Log Contracts.

At its core, Mutiny Wallet isn't just a bitcoin wallet; I see it as some sort of a manifesto, a challenge to the status quo of mobile apps, and a testament to what can be achieved when technology is built from the ground up with the user's interests in mind - especially maximizing freedom.

# Zeus: The most flexible mobile Lightning wallet?

The Zeus wallet has been in development since 2019. At first, it served primarily as an interface to your own Lightning node, running on a (home) server, but later it added the ability to run a lightning node on a mobile device, similar to the Breez wallet, for example. Does this place the Zeus wallet among the second-generation Lightning wallets?

Lightning wallets are a pretty tough nut to crack. Compared to on-chain wallets, they face different challenges.

For an on-chain wallet, perhaps a "keychain" is a better term - all a Bitcoin on-chain wallet needs to do is hold and use keys and create transactions with them. There are no Bitcoins stored in an on-chain "keychain", just keys to unlock coins that are held in a public database. With the Lightning wallet comes the need to worry about the channels and their state. Thus, the wallet holds a lot of other information that is necessary besides the keys - channels and their state (last commit transaction, node keys), revocation keys, and so on. This data needs to be backed up or this problem needs to be solved some other way.

In addition, other issues need to be resolved. They must take care of the management of channels and solve the situation of receiving sats when there's not enough incoming channel capacity. In addition, unlike on-chain payment, the receiver must be online (and sign a new channel state) when receiving payment, which is a challenge if the user has a mobile device that is not online all the time.

And finally, it's the user experience - should the end-user deal with which coins are in a lightning channel and which are only at a regular on-chain address, or should the wallet show a unified balance?

The Zeus wallet made many of these decisions differently than other second-generation wallets like Breez and Phoenix. Bitcoin is an open-source project, and diversity is desirable in this case. However, that doesn't mean this wallet (or any other wallet for that matter) is suitable for everyone.

## Connecting Zeus wallet to your own node

The Zeus wallet originally served as an app connected to your node on RaspBlitz, BTCPayserver, NODL, Umbrel or other similar service that lets you create and operate your own Lightning node. It supports Core Lightning or LND based nodes. The most common use case is that you use your Zeus app to scan a Lightning invoice and the wallet app would tell your node to pay the invoice. You can also open channels, receive sats (both on-chain and over lightning).

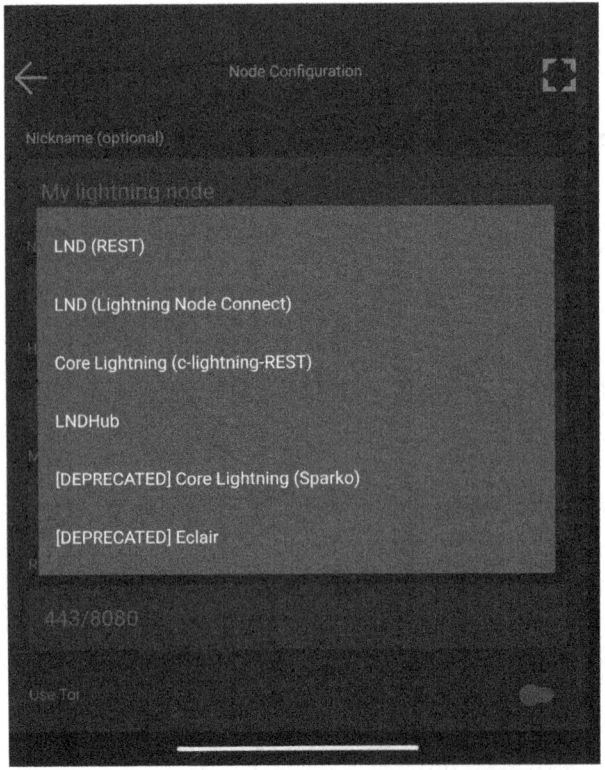

*Setting up a connection to a custom Lightning node*

To this end, it is a rather unique application, the only alternative to which is perhaps the now defunct Zap wallet. If you're running your own node, definitely check out Zeus. I would expect to connect directly over the Lightning network using [Project Commando](), which would simplify access since there's no need to open or forward TCP ports. I hope this functionality will come at some point as well.

# Lightning node on the device

Non-custodial second-generation wallets like Breez and Phoenix run some form of Lightning node directly on the device. Phoenix runs a minimalist node that performs all operations related to keys and balance, but uses the wallet authors' node for routing, for example. Breez wallet works similarly to Zeus with embedded node - it runs its own lnd node on the smartphone itself. This has the advantage of better privacy and sovereignty, but the disadvantage of having to synchronize the state of the Bitcoin blockchain (using the Neutrino extension) and synchronizing the Lightning graph to find the optimal path. A common user experience is that if they have a prepaid data plan and open their wallet after a not using it for a while, their local node will consume all their data.

*The first thing after creating a wallet on a local node on the device will be to synchronize with the network. This is not exactly a great user experience, unfortunately.*

Zeus is in a similar position. Once the wallet is created, it syncs and waiting for the node to start Syncing will keep you waiting for subsequent launches as well. After a week of inactivity, it took almost half a minute to launch (fast device, fast data connection). One can enable background sync, but I think this syncing will deter many users, especially if they want to use Zeus in their store to accept payments and it's not happening everyday.

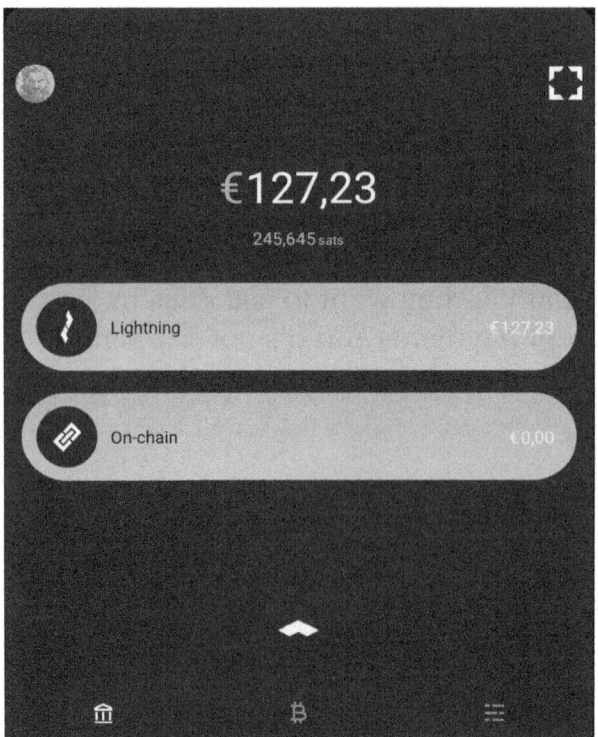

*Figure: Zeus does not have a unified balance - some of your funds are in Lightning, some are on-chain. It also doesn't provide an easy way to "swap" between these balances. With on-chain funds you can open a channel with someone, you can manually close a Lightning channel to get on-chain funds, but there's no easy way to use some swap service like Boltz, which allows you to keep your channels and just swap one way or another.*

The Breez wallet does run a local node, but it has a unified balance (which is always in channels) and has a hardcoded Lightning Service Provider (or Liquidity provider) - all channels the wallet opens with Breez's node.

Zeus gives you full control over your local lnd node - you can create new channels, and make onchain payments directly from an integrated on-chain wallet. Even so, it has built-in support for Lightning service providers, including the default Olympus provider, which will open a channel to you, if needed.

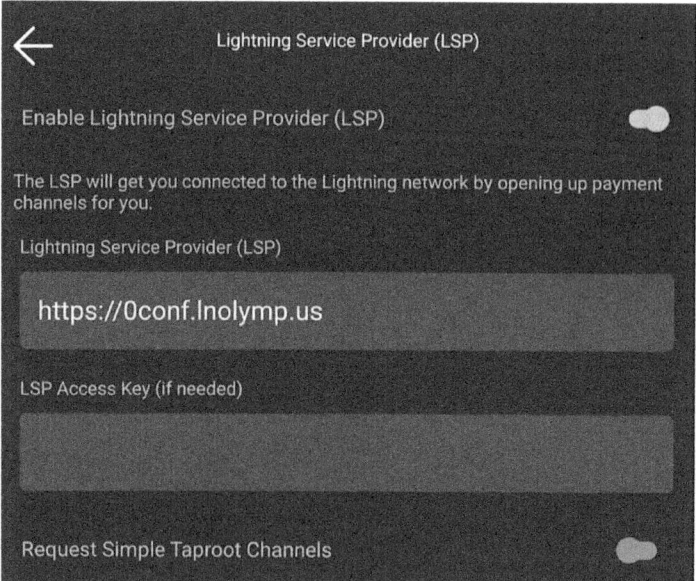

*Figure: Lightning service provider settings. The default provider is Olympus operated by the wallet manufacturers.*

## Accepting payments

If we want to accept satoshi via Lightning after installation, it will work automatically. We also have full control over what the invoice looks like. We can send it via NFC (for contactless transfer of the invoice to the phone – no camera for QR codes needed!), or receive it via NFC (using the lnurl protocol, to enable contactless Lightning payments such as with NFC payment cards). We can also accept funds on-chain, but unlike Lightning wallets Phoenix and Breez, the balance will end up in a separate balance.

*Figure: Displaying a unified payment request using a QR code, a unified URI, or NFC. Zeus also allows us to create a pure Lightning or onchain code and even a Lightning address.*

It is also possible to accept via a non-custodial Lightning address using the ZeusPay service based on the zaplocker project. This technology uses so-called HODL invoices, where the service providing the invoices provides hashes to which it does not have a "key" (prehash). Thus, the client creates a payment path when making a payment, but it has an expiration time of 24 hours. If the wallet is open within these 24 hours, it receives via the Nostr protocol information about the individual lightning invoices that are waiting to be processed, and the wallet creates the last part of the path and, by passing the keys, settles (and thus accepts) them.

The problem with this approach is that the payment path has funds locked for 24 hours, with no one being rewarded for this Bitcoin lock along the way. Thus, some wallets like Mutiny block payments from the Zeus wallet with such a long expiration. While this solution is secure in terms of storing Bitcoins, it is not very practical (payment success depends on opening the wallet on mobile within 24 hours) and unnecessarily congests the network, thus creating contention between developers, routing node providers and users. I recommend using some other tool for Lightning address - for example npub.cash with your favorite Cashu mint. This project also uses the Nostr protocol, it will give you the lightning address, but for the time until payment is received you have to trust the ecash mint you choose.

# Sending sats

Sending is similar - we have quite a lot of options, but we have to have a balance either in Lightning or on-chain depending on which way we want to send the funds. Again, we have the option to use NFC.

Even when sending, it shows that the user is in control in this wallet - we can see exactly what happens when we pay.

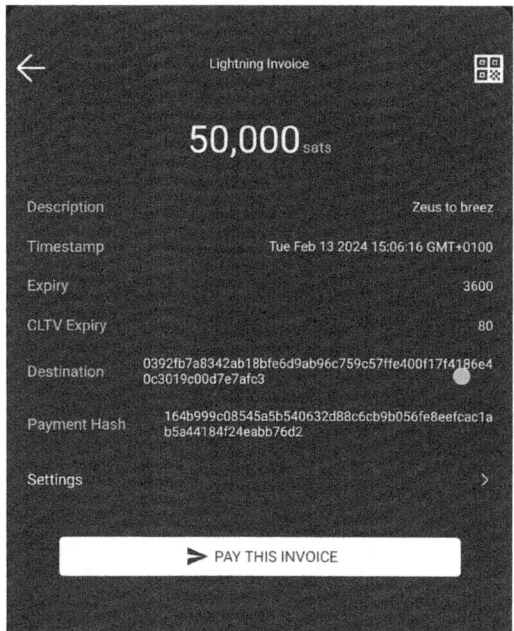

*Image: we can see detailed information about the Lightning invoice - in addition to the description and amount, we can also see the timestamp, expiration date, destination node address or payment hash of the transaction.*

Personally, I would welcome the integration of some swap service and the possibility of a unified balance.

## Channel Management

Unlike Phoenix or Breez, but similar to the Blixt wallet for example, you have full control over the channels. If you're using Olympus LSP, you might get automatically opened channels, but you can also open channels with whomever you want.

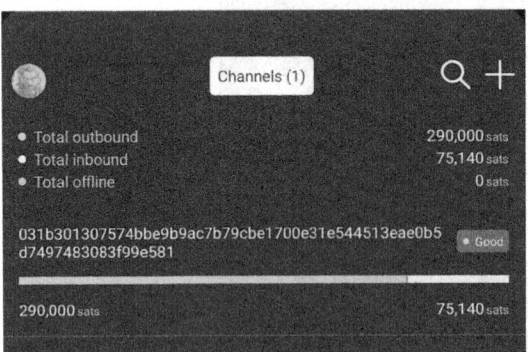

*Figure: List of open channels. We can see the capacity to send and receive - both overall and per channel.*

When we open a channel, we have several options - the wallet even allows coin control, so we can choose which UTXOs we want to use and whether we want to use their entire balance.

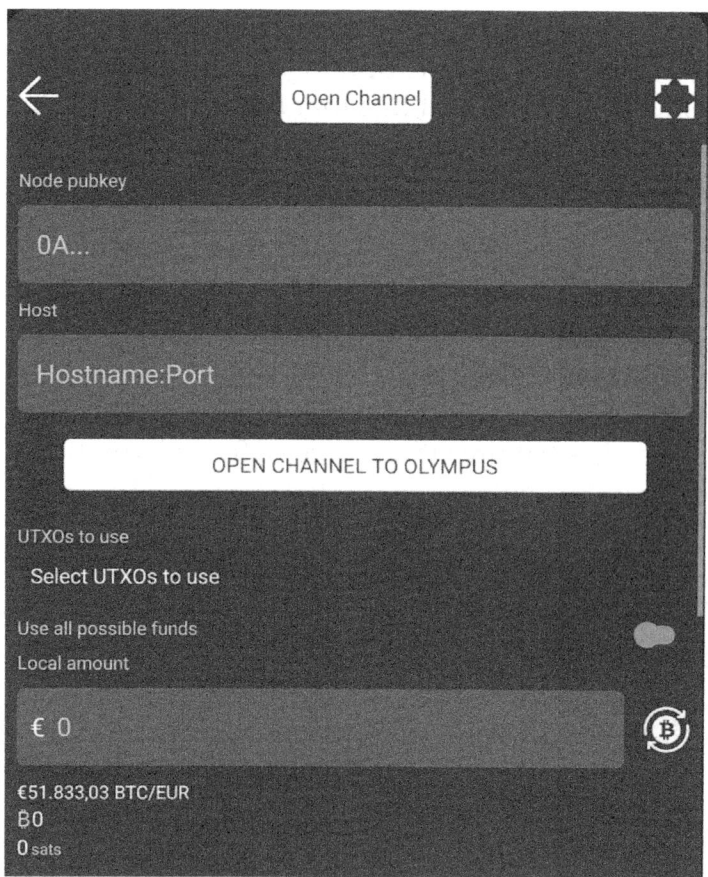

*Figure: Interface to open the channel. We choose the node we want to open the channel with (using the public key), its address (we can choose to pre-populate this data for the Olympus LSP), choose the UTXOs we want to open the channel with, and choose the amount.*

When opening (and likewise for on-chain payments) we have the option to choose a fee. Unlike other wallets, I like that the fees that are shown come from the mempool.space project, which I personally prefer, because it makes sense to me.

If any other wallet shows me some recommended fees, I usually open mempool.space anyway, because otherwise I don't know where the wallet got the fees from. This is not a problem with Zeus, because it attributes the source of fee information to mempool.space.

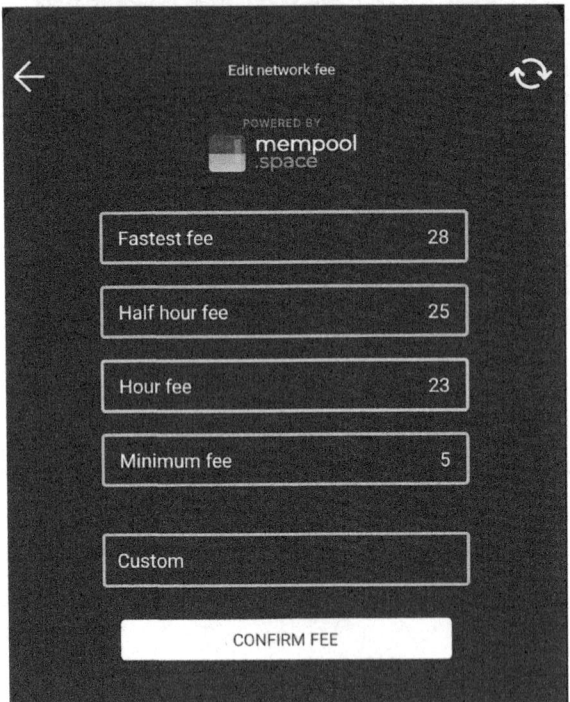

*Figure: Fee options in sats/vB uses mempool.space as source. Of course, you can also choose your own fee.*

Once the opening transaction is created, just wait for the block in which the funding channel transaction will be included to be mined, and you can use it with lightning.

## Settings

Compared to other wallets, Zeus has a lot of settings where you can customize virtually anything. Of course, there is the choice of fiat currency for display and calculations, but also the choice of language.

You should also make backups. The backup is created similarly to the Phoenix and Breez wallets and is made up of a mnemonic seed backup (24 words in the case of Zeus).

*Figure: Interface to back up the wallet using a mnemonic seed*

The more knowledgeable among you will immediately think of the question of the status of the channels. Zeus only does static channel backup, to Olympus servers. These are encrypted by seed, but do not contain the channel state, so when restoring the wallet, you can only ask the counterparties to close the channels - you can't do it yourself. Here it is important to think about how you trust the counterparties you are opening channels with, to comply with this request.

## Point of sale – accepting payments

One of the fairly unique things about Zeus is the built-in module for accepting payments (Point of Sale). Virtually anyone can accept Lightning payments through any wallet - just add up the amount, enter it (possibly in local fiat currency which will be converted by the wallet to sats amount), and show the Lightning invoice QR code. This is possible if you are, for example, a "freelancer" - a massage therapist, have your own coffee shop, where you also work or accept payments in person yourself.

You need something better when you don't want to have a wallet with private keys on the premises or handed over to employees. These wallets can also send money out. This will prevent theft of equipment, mishandling, and the like.

Larger operations can use devices based on an open-source PoS service built on the [btcpayserver](btcpayserver) project - either by installing it themselves, or as a hosted service. Or you can use a commercial service such as the one from [Confirmo](Confirmo).

Between receiving to your own wallet and using a server-based service (whether custom or hosted as a service), there is a room for non-custodial solutions that run directly on the device but are somehow protected against theft. The first innovation of this type was the Breez wallet, which has its own PoS terminal. It allows you to set an "admin password" which is needed when you want to change any settings, or want to send money out of the wallet, or view seed. The common operator of the terminal (employee) can only receive, but cannot send transactions.

The downside of Breez's solution is the inability to accept on-chain transactions in this PoS mode, and the limit of the Breez wallet itself at 4M satoshi, which will not be enough for some establishments.

Zeus has similar payment terminal functionality. You can set a password or PIN that is required for sending.

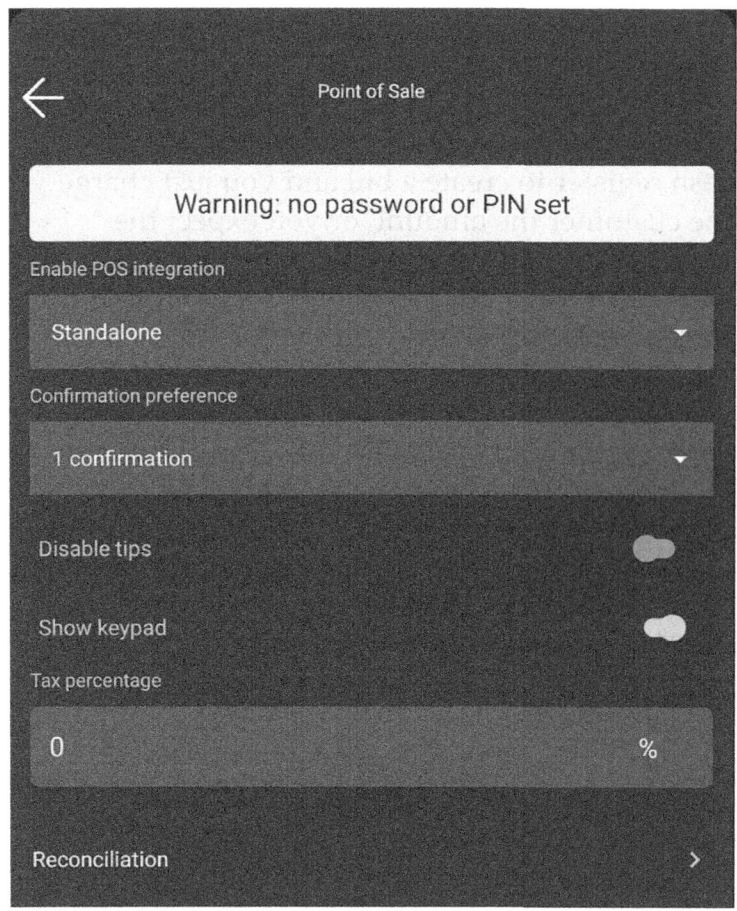

*Figure: Basic settings of the module for accepting payments. You can choose whether for on-chain payments the terminal will wait for a confirmation, or if it is enough to see an attempt at payment that is not yet confirmed.*

You can also create individual products in the settings. And this is where the different types of PoS terminal usage get a bit mixed up. There are two possible approaches - either you use a classic cash register to create a bill and you just charge the customer the amount, or you expect the terminal to charge individual items. Let's take the example of card payments that is similar to the first case. The cash register calculates how much you have to pay after the cashier enters all the products you are paying for. Then the cashier enters the amount calculated on the cash register on the payment terminal screen to accept card payment in that amount. And the payment terminal just tells the cashier whether the payment went through or not. With some terminals, you don't even have to enter anything and the cash register can send the amount to the card payment acceptance module and check the status of the payment automatically.

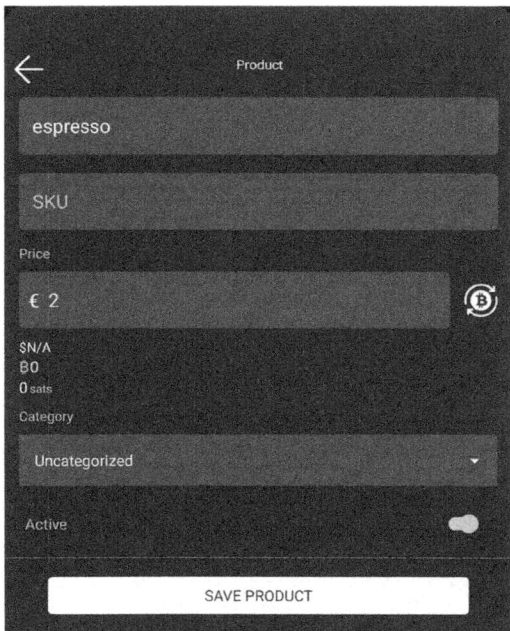

*Figure: Creating items with amounts that can be "added" to a bill before a payment request is created*

The second option is that the terminal to receive payments does the job of the cash register. This is useful if you only accept one type of payment, or if you can use the bill from this terminal to accept another type of payment. For example, if you are a sole proprietorship selling goods or services when a client visits you in person, it is nice to be able to click the individual products and services directly in the Lightning wallet and click to create a Lightning invoice with the amount it calculates.

Even if the customer will end up paying cash, you don't need to have a separate price list and calculator, but it will calculate the amount you will collect from the customer. Of course, the legal requirements for accepting payments might not be addressed by this terminal and you must resolve them differently, if this is the case.

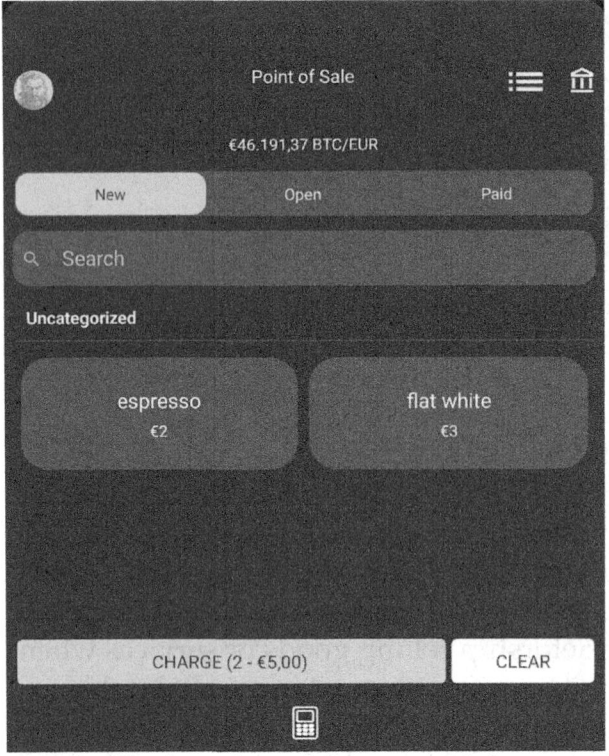

*Figure: The interface of the terminal for accepting payments. We can see the items we can add "to cart".*

If we enable the "Show Keypad" option in the terminal settings, we can also charge the amount directly - so we use the "card terminal" mode I was talking about - we only create an invoice with the amount, we don't have to worry about the items themselves. The cash register outside of Zeus (or the cashier in their head) calculates how much the client must pay and if he wants to pay in bitcoin, we open the "keypad" and enter the amount in fiat currency:

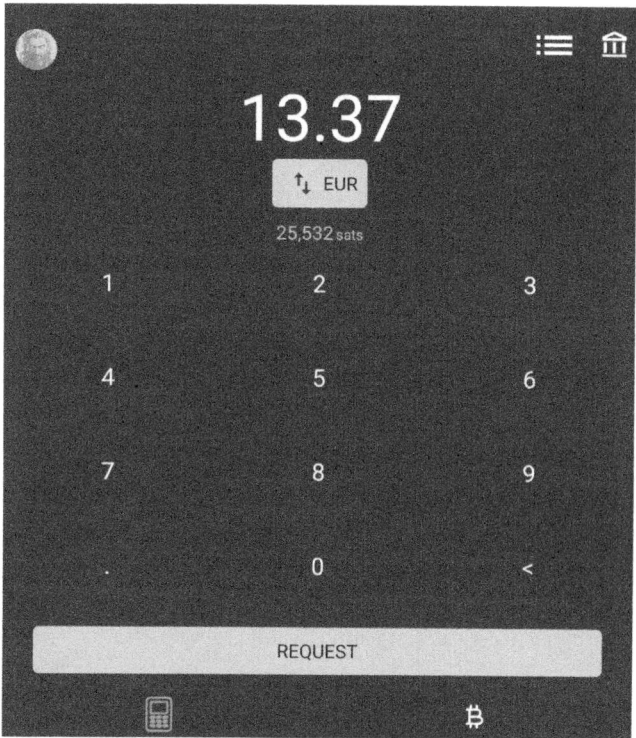

Image: keyboard where we can enter the amount (in fiat currency, but also in satoshi) and request payment of a specific amount, without the need to select products.

Compared to the Breez wallet terminal, we can accept on-chain payments, just like Lightning payments (but the on-chain payment functionality can also be disabled). By the way, Breez allows you to accept on-chain payments via a swap service (using the Receive via Bitcoin Address option), but this option is not integrated into the payment terminal.

Unlike the Breez wallet payment terminal, in Zeus PoS we see a list of payments - new, open and paid. If we want to see which payment has gone through, we can see it in the history.

## Conclusion

Zeus is a great choice if you want to use your own node and connect to it. It will allow you to pay, receive payments and do it all in a user-friendly way from your mobile device.

If you are interested in accepting payments in your store or small business, the PoS module can also be an interesting option to accept Lightning - not only with QR codes, but also with various NFC cards and the like.

If you only want to use Lightning, have full control over private keys, but don't want to worry about channels, figuring out how to swap your balance between Lightning and on-chain, and basically only need to send and receive, other wallets will probably be better suited for you.

# Expanding the Lightning network to serve billions – a quick-win strategy

As Bitcoin blocks are being filled and fees rise astronomically, it has become too expensive to open channels for many day-to-day use-cases. In this blog I want to build a case for expanding the Lightning network beyond the bloated Bitcoin time-chain (also called a blockchain), to give people more options.

First, let's look at how Lightning actually uses Bitcoin timechain. Lightning is a separate payment network that allows to send and receive Bitcoin. It uses a cryptoanarchist strategy of "prepaid fine" and some clever game-theory to make sure no one cheats. In case of Lightning, the cheating would be trying to settle a channel balance with an outdated state, which would be punished by an on-chain transaction that takes the cheater's whole channel balance.

Lightning has different properties than Bitcoin time-chain – better privacy, lower fees, instant settlement. Also, it is non-custodial – we are sending real Bitcoin, not a derivative (each channel close transaction settles the correct balance on-chain, but you do not need to close channels to settle).

There are two problems with traditional use of Lightning and both relate to scaling. One is that for many, the on-chain fee is already prohibitive. People living on $1 a day or less can't pay several dollars just to have a (small) channel open to them.

Another problem is the real capacity. Let's say we want to onboard one hundred million more users. Assuming a channel opening transaction of cca 150vB, we can realistically open around 5000 channels per each block, which would take around 138 days assuming Bitcoin time-chain would not be used for anything else. And in this case, the fees would be extremely high anyway.

## Expanding Lightning

It is possible to open Lightning channels without the implicit Bitcoin backing. These are called **hosted channels or unbacked channels**. For example, I can open a channel with someone, use it to access the whole Lightning network and then settle however I want – with cash, it can be a credit account, etc. What is important is that the receiver of such transaction does not need to know that the transaction happened via hosted channel, they receive Bitcoin through the channels that they have opened.

This allows us to use different accounting methods than Bitcoin on-chain transactions, if the unit of account is the same.

One nice real-world example of this approach is using Cashu or Fedimint protocols, which are based on a technology called chaumian e-cash, to settle Lightning invoices. Another example would be to use Liquid network with a swap service to do the same. For example Aqua Wallet uses atomic swaps between Liquid on-chain and Lightning. You still need to settle a liquid transaction (blocks are generated once per minute), so the transactions are not instant, but there is no need to open a channel for each user on Bitcoin main time-chain.

## Using Liquid to expand Lightning

An obvious and super easy way would be to use the Liquid side-chain not using atomic swaps, but for opening channels. Before you start with "it is not decentralized, …", yes, I agree and I do not like it that much either. But bear with me, this is still **much** better than the custodial wallets! Imagine a consumer wallet like Phoenix or Breez, allowing you to choose opening channels on Liquid instead of Bitcoin timechain, with much lower fees.

People could run HOSTED CHANNELS between Liquid and Bitcoin timechains, essentially making money on bridging – this could be even provided by the provider of the wallet to earn some additional revenue. Please note that hosted channels in this case are **trustless**, it is a channel between two nodes of the same node operator (each operator implicitly trusts himself or herself). End-users would choose if they want channels on Bitcoin timechain for higher fees and higher security, or if it is a "coffee budget" that is not very important. What is crucial here is that merchants would receive normal Bitcoin, because the payment would be routed trustlessly through the bridge. The Lightning network would expand and use different backing mechanisms that are suited for different users. Merchants want "real bitcoin", customers want low fees. And we can have both.

There can also be a "one-click" conversion tool, for example in times of lower fees on Bitcoin chain, which would just create a lightning payment through the bridge to oneself, opening an incoming channel in the process. We could have a feature saying "when the value of Bitcoin is over $100, route to Bitcoin chain automatically, opening a channel on the way". This consolidates incoming channels, improves security when it matters, but allows for cheap and fast on-boarding. It could also allow batched channel opening – when the provider sees that the fees are low, it could ask you to cooperate in a transaction that opens multiple channels in one transaction.

## Advantages for users

Users would get easier onboarding and lower fees. The user interface could be kept simple, there is no different invoice format or anything, it is just Lightning, backed by bridged coins. It can be entirely opt-in and would show people the power of Bitcoin without the initial fees and frustration. Liquid is not very decentralized I do not own any L-BTC, but I believe this could improve user experience.

## Advantages for merchants

Merchants can decide to receive only Bitcoin backed by real Lightning channels. To do this, they do not need to do anything. They get access to customers who opened these Liquid-backed channels for free. Less fees paid to miners – more money to be spent for coffee in your coffee shop!

On the other hand, if they do not have incoming liquidity, they could decide to allow automatic incoming channel opening on Liquid (Phoenix-style) and then consolidate once a week (or even swap-out to onchain hardware-wallet-protected address).

Merchants do not want business to go down, because the customers are hesitant to fund their wallets in times of high fees.

## Advantages for wallet providers

Wallet providers can keep more of the channel creation fee for themselves if they do not have to pay miners. They can also earn fees on bridging and swapping balances from Liquid-backed to Bitcoin-backed. This whole operation is trustless.

They can also get more users by lowering the fees and making their project more attractive. Integrating with some parts of the wider ecosystem – Nostr for zaps, podcasting 2.0, … – requires low fees, the entry fees cannot be too high.

## Advantages for Bitcoin and Lightning

In money, network effects are everything. Reducing friction enables on-boarding more users, on-boarding more users expands value of the network and that pumps your bags. Let's do it!

## How to do it?

To build a bridge, you need to run two **core lightning** instances (one on Bitcoin, one on Liquid) and create a **hosted channel**. There is no code to write, core lightning already supports Liquid. Set the fees, you are good to go.

The only thing would be to allow lightning for consumer end-user wallets. Here unfortunately, there is no good Liquid support, because the end-user wallets do not run core lightning, but either lnd or acinq's lightweight Lightning implementation. It should not be too difficult to add.

## Why not Litecoin, ...?

For this to work the unit of account needs to be the same. Litecoin also has a Lightning implementation, but it sends Litecoins, not Bitcoin. So there would need to be unit of account conversion, which introduces exchange rates and a lot of unnecessary friction. Also, we do not want to teach new Bitcoiners to have Litecoin.

## But isn't it custodial?

No, it is not. Let me explain the security design and risks that differ to Bitcoin timechain-backed channels. Feel free to skip this part if you are not into technical details of Bitcoin and Liquid.

- You need to trust the backing on Liquid chain. This is not ideal, Bitcoin is protected by huge hashpower, Liquid is protected by quite a large, but still limited "federation". Cheating would be obvious though and many different entities would have to cooperate to steal your "coffee money".

Liquid still has nodes and timechain, so you cannot simply take coins without knowing the opening transaction's two multisig private keys.

- The biggest threat is transaction censorship by validators. This can happen, but also note, that you can get out using Lightning, without an on-chain transaction. So both your channel counterparty and Liquid would need to censor.

- Another threat is Liquid stealing the BTC (intentionally or unintentionally) by releasing the locked BTC from the peg-in multisig. Again, this would be clearly visible and much bigger issue than my coffee money. Also, these coins would probably be immediately tainted on Bitcoin timechain.

- No one needs to trust the hosted channel and the bridge. The hosted channel is between bridge operator's two Lightning nodes – essentially the bridge operator receives L-BTC through one channel and sends BTC through another channel of theirs. This L-BTC<->BTC exchange does not need channel backing, because it is atomic and trustless. The bridge will collect fees for this service, because they probably need to rebalance from time to time, but that's it. You as a user (or your lightning wallet) can find the path with the cheapest bridge – sometimes even with negative fees if you help them rebalance.

- The merchants that want Bitcoin-backed Lightning balance do not have to deal with nor even know about the fact that the payment originated through Liquid. The payment arrives through one of their open channels, if they do not support Liquid, there is no difference.

So basically the only entity to trust here is the Liquid federation for validating transactions and maintaining the bridge. And even this trust requirement can be greatly reduced, because it cannot be easily targeted. This expansion of Lightning actually reduces the risk of the federation multisig, because there is now another way out – through the bridge.

Creating these Lightning bridges (unlike in many other projects and cross-chain bridges) is completely trustless, decentralized and there is a competitive market for it – bridge operators compete on fees and liquidity.

## How does it work in practice?

The bridge is trustless, because for both sides it is just a lightning channel. So it is trustless the same way normal lightning payment routing is trustless. It has to be operated by the same entity, because the bridge is not backed by coins, but both paths to and from the bridge are.

Example: Let's say you are paying a lightning invoice, the path to the recipient node has channels backed by one Bitcoin channel and you yourself have a channel backed by Liquid (BTW: You can have both Liquid and Bitcoin-backed channels and you can partially use both, even for the same payment!). From the point of view of lightning, this is one network (using the same unit of account). Your wallet ("Liquid side") would create a route. It sees the bridge just as another lightning channel, so if the fees for routing are OK, it will be included in the created route.

When the route is created, the invoice is being paid. The recipient publishes the prehash down the way as normal lightning payment and the HTLCs are slowly removed (because the prehash is revealed), starting from the recipient and going along the path to the sender. As money flows through, the claim (represented by prehash to commited funds) reaches the bitcoin side of the bridge. The channel that constitutes the bridge is not "real" (it is a virtual/hosted channel) and because the funds belong to the same entity, it does not matter how is it split – 0.1BTC/0.2LBTC vs. 0.2BTC/0.1LBTC split does not matter to the operator, because they own both sides, so they are 0.3(L)BTC net worth, split somehow.

After the prehash arrives at the bridge from "Bitcoin side", meaning someone claimed the payment amount from the bitcoin side of the bridge. In order for the bridge operator to keep their net worth, they will just give the prehash to the other side of the bridge (it's their node), basically passing it "for free" to the other lightning daemon. And that will use it to claim the precommited amount through the liquid side of the bridge and it's channel to the liquid part of the network, ultimately being paid by the sender.

If Bob is the recipient, the balance of the bridge changes from:

```
Bob ->0.1BTC Bridge < hosted ch. > 0.2LBTC -> Alice
```

into

```
Bob ->0.2BTC Bridge < hosted ch. > 0.1LBTC -> Alice
```

Bob is paid, Alice is paying, the balances of BTC vs LBTC side of bridge change, but net amount is the same (actually higher because the routing fees are paid to the bridge).

## Conclusion

We have it in our power to expand Lightning network way beyond the Bitcoin timechain. We can allow end-users to make their choices of backing and dispute resolution. We keep most of the properties (limited supply, hard money), empowering users and bringing more value to the network.

# Lightning network – the payment network of the Internet

Although most bitcoin users look primarily at price and earnings, bitcoin has delivered much more than "just" digital gold. Even though altcoiners often criticize Bitcoin for being "slow" because blocks are created every 10 minutes on average, a payment network has been created over the Bitcoin protocol that will put any altcoin to shame.

The Lightning network has payments with instant finality, no need to wait for any confirmation by anyone else (there is no miner, or validator to wait for). The network is also known for its low payment fees – in fact, the network nodes compete with each other on fees specifically, so prices are driven down by long-term competitive pressure.

At the moment Lightning is mainly used for Bitcoin payments between users. However, the potential of Lightning is much greater. I realized this when I came across a payment terminal that didn't support Lightning payments in a coffee shop. I could have paid with Bitcoin with a high fee or some altcoin, but I don't own any that was supported. Thanks to the existence of **instant non-KYC exchanges** and the **law of cryptocurrency isomorphism**, we can use any cryptocurrency to pay, even if we don't have it directly.

# Lightning is the ideal payment protocol

If we wanted to use another cryptocurrency like Monero or Ethereum in this way, we would have two problems. For Monero, the basic problem would be that we would need to wait for the block to be mined – the exchange needs to wait for at least one confirmation, otherwise it could be a victim of a double-spend attack. The average Monero block is 2 minutes, but it could easily be that the block doesn't arrive for several minutes. In addition, with a busier network, our transaction may not appear in the next block. If we are standing in a cafe paying a bill, the cafe will not see the Litecoin transaction, for example, until our Monero payment is included in the block. Some exchanges even wait ten blocks (20 minutes) until the Monero is spendable.

Block time is shorter on Ethereum, although sometimes it can take a minute to include a transaction, for example, the fees are usually high.

Lightning has predictably low fees and no need to wait for any blocks.

# Searching for the ideal payment protocol of the internet

Lightning can thus be thought of as a basic payment protocol through which we can send value over the Internet. If I have a classic payment card (such as Visa, Mastercard, …) in euros, I pay with it in Paraguay, not only the sending of fiat currency will pass through the payment protocol, but there might be several currency exchanges going on in the background. I pay with the balance in euros, it has to be converted first to dollars so that the recipient will receive the guaraní (because there is no direct PYG/EUR pair).

# Liquidity

And here comes another feature of Lightning – it uses Bitcoin, which is extremely liquid. While liquidity is not directly related to market capitalization, we can infer the approximate size of networks from it. Ethereum has a market capitalization of about a third of Bitcoin's capitalization. Then there is BNB (Binance coin) and Solana, which are around 6%. And then nothing (I don't count stablecoins, those are dollars, just in a different payment network – and they are liquid enough). So the distribution is as we expect it to be for the networks following network effect laws – it follows the power law.

If Liquidity is important (which it is if there are exchanges going on), there is no better option in cryptocurrency world than Bitcoin – the native currency of the Lightning network.

## Absence of dirty coins

Another advantage of Lightning is that coins have no history and thus are fungible. There are no dirty coins in Lightning, they are all the same. This is a key feature for a payment network because it needs to be software-based and should be predictable – we don't want a payment to stop because someone didn't like the coins along the way. This is fortunately not a problem with Lightning.

## Programmability

Instant, inexpensive, "clean" payments using a liquid asset as a transported unit of account. What else? Programmability and multi-chain capability. I covered multi-chain capability in the previous chapter, so let's look at programmability. With it, we can, for example, do atomic swaps – that is, a payment between different chains that either occurs in its entirety or not at all.

If we look at the credit card example – a number of things occurred along the way. I used euros from my bank account, euros were exchanged for USD on an exchange, USD was exchanged for PYG on another exchange, and the merchant's account received exactly the amount of PYG he requested. In addition, no one can lose out on exchange rate differences.

Exchange rates usually cost the client from 0% to 1%, receiving payment fees are 1%-5% and paid by the merchant. At least in terms of pricing, we have room to innovate. However, the fees also reflect what can go wrong along the way. If the "payment path" takes too long to create and confirm, it must be more expensive to exchange the currencies from one to another. The longer it takes to confirm, the more the exchange rate can move (and thus someone gets a free exchange rate option).

If the payment is not atomic, it translates to higher the fees for the payment itself (even if there is no exchange of one currency for another). What does it mean for a payment path to be atomic? Let's look at what it means for the payment to not be atomic: For example, it could be that funds are deducted from the sender's balance, but don't arrive to the receiver, or vice versa. What can happen is that the payment is indeed confirmed, but it is eventually discovered that there has been credit card fraud. In this case, the merchant saw the payment confirmation, has given the customer the goods or services in exchange for the card payment, but the payment is later reverted, and the merchant will not actually receive the money.

Atomic payment means that everything happens as a whole – no part of the transaction can happen on its own, but either the whole transaction happens, or no part of the transaction happens.

Lightning itself is atomic, but thanks to programmability, Bitcoin exchanges over Lightning for another cryptocurrency can also be atomic. With some "plumbing", so can hedges to other (fiat) currencies of the world be atomic. If Bitcoins left my Lightning wallet, Litecoins will surely arrive to the recipient.

# Even better programmability

The programmability in Lightning goes much further, however. Rene Pickhardt and I wrote a paper in June 2019 about **Lightning Discreet Log Contracts**. With this technology, it is possible to essentially store a "smart contract" in the Lightning channel, whereby we can, for example, hedge the exchange rate of Bitcoin against the dollar and effectively hold a dollar balance in the Lightning channel – even with interest.

This idea was implemented by the **10101** project, which allowed you to have a Lightning wallet with both a dollar and a bitcoin balance at the same time, and you could pay with the dollar balance. This dollar balance was not represented by a stablecoin though – it was sats and a short position, which together create a stable dollar value. There was no Tether or any other third-party token involved in this process.
While the project did switch from direct Lightning channels to simplified DLC channels that can't route payments, paying from them using HTLC and atomic swaps is technically feasible and relatively easy to implement in the future.

Either atomic swap technology or Lightning DLC will allow us to implement what card-based payment networks do – the payee wants a balance in guarani, I have some euros in Lightning channels. The payee thus creates a Lightning invoice that includes an atomic change of satoshi to guarani as part of the payment, I retrieve it and pay the necessary amount of satoshi, but I do so by stepping out of the position that fixed their euro value for me. I paid in "euros", the "guaraní" came in, but only sats went through the network, because nothing else can natively go through the Lightning network.

Bitcoin as a universal currency (money, digital scarcity) is an instant universal means of payment, but we don't have to encounter it if we don't want to – and we can still take advantage of its unique properties.

Of course, I think people should encounter it – anything else than Bitcoin is a huge risk these days, especially fiat. But people can still benefit from the Lightning payment network, even if they have not swallowed the orange pill yet.

## Second generation backend software

Following the first-generation Lightning wallets came second-generation wallets like Phoenix and Breez, which unify Lightning and on-chain balance, automatically open channels, provide swap services, and simplify Lightning usage to two buttons: "Send" and "Receive".

The same thing is starting to happen with backend software. For example, **Blockstream's Greenlight** service allows you to leave most of the complex operations like blockchain synchronization, payment routing, and the like to the cloud service (built on a "core lightning" node), but leave all the operations with private keys to the end device. This service is used by the Breez SDK project, which makes it possible to build Lightning applications without having to run the entire Lightning node on the end device but keeping the user sovereignty and ownership of private keys with the end user, in trustless way.

Another interesting project is **phoenixd**, which is a relatively tiny Lightning node that works much like the Phoenix wallet – you receive and send from a unified balance, and phoenixd opens channels for you if needed (for a fee). Accepting a Lightning payment into your app is one simple API call, and phoenixd handles everything for you.

If 10101 or similar service gets this level of programmable backend access, we would get the ability to own any form of value in a Lightning channel – or another technology that is atomic-swappable over lightning. We can also send this balance anywhere, even if there is nothing else but sats sent over the lightning network itself.

## Conclusion

Thanks to the features of Lightning, I think that Lightning will be the protocol for settling (clearing) payments even in cases where individual users will not want to use Bitcoin for the payment itself – either as recipients or senders. For many use cases, the protocol will even be invisible to users. A player of an online RPG game buys a new orange spacesuit for his character, pays for it with his credit card, the fiat currency gets atomically converted into Bitcoin, sent via Lightning to the seller of that orange spacesuit, who uses a service to accept payments with the payout to an Indian bank account in rupees.

Most of the way, the payment goes through the payment channel in the form of Bitcoins (or sats), atomically, but the input and output can be a completely different currency and payment network.

Lightning will thus become a universal transport system for transferring value anywhere on the planet. Of course, Bitcoiners would prefer that all transactions begin and end in Bitcoins. But there is no technical or philosophical reason for such an ideological constraint on the Lightning protocol – people choose the money they want and are ready for – and sort of also what they deserve.

# Conclusion

Bitcoin has created a great decentralized unit of account and an asset that can be truly owned. The Lightning network leverages this innovation and adds a fast payment network that has lower fees for most payments and no need to store transactions. The combination of these two technologies is the foundation of the parallel financial system of the future.

*Image: Bitcoin has created digital gold, the Lightning network protocol enables the financial communication of the entire world.*

The Lightning network is an important innovation in the Bitcoin family of protocols. It enables instant payments with low fees, no history risk and sufficient privacy. The ecosystem around the Lightning protocol is in its second epoch of development - the hardest birth pains are behind it, it is developing and growing. If you use Bitcoin, you should also use the Lightning network.

# Bonus: Bitcoin in a high fee environment

From time to time, fees on the Bitcoin network will go up and transactions can cost up to tens of dollars. This is due to the Bitcoin network's limit on block size. There are several perspectives on this - from the fact that Bitcoin is unusable at the first layer with such fees and thus does not meet the properties of peer-to-peer electronic cash, to the fact that the fees are still low and will not be enough in the future as a reward to miners to secure the network with sufficient hashrate.

In this chapter, we look at the different options for what we can do in a high fee environment.

# What are the current fees?

To know what fees to use in the first place, we need to know how the fees work and how does the current fee market look like. A scarce resource in blocks is called blockspace, which is how many bytes can fit in a block. This limit is currently set at 1MB, although not all bytes count equally (the detailed workings are beyond the scope of this chapter, but in principle some bytes of so-called witness data are discounted). Newly created transactions arrive in a so-called mempool, which is maintained by each node and is a list of transactions not yet confirmed on chain. These may be replaced by other transactions in some circumstances before they are mined. The miner looks at his mempool and selects the transactions so that his reward is as high as possible. A nice visualisation of a mempool is, for example, mempool.space.

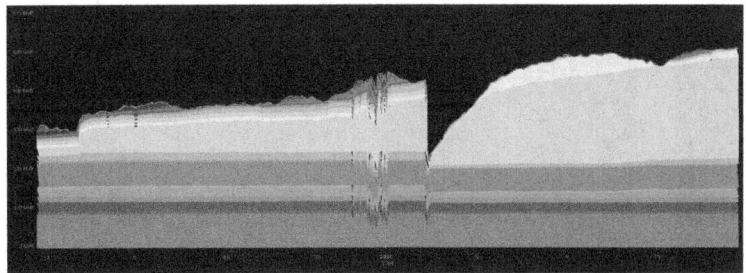

*Image: Visualisation of mempool size by mempool.space. The visualization shows two weeks in this case.*

In the chart we can see the amount of each transaction along with the "unit fee", i.e. how much sat per vB transaction pays. The vB stands for virtual byte and accounts for the discount of witness data. Higher up on the chart are transactions that pay a higher fee and each new block "bites off" the chart - mostly from the top, but it doesn't have to be that way because the transaction fee can either be paid by another transaction or some miners can be paid outside the blockchain. It is thus possible to "bite" from somewhere other than the top, but in most cases it is from the top. If we see the structure of this chart, we can see how many unconfirmed transactions are in this particular mempool and how long it would take for the miners to mine our transaction.

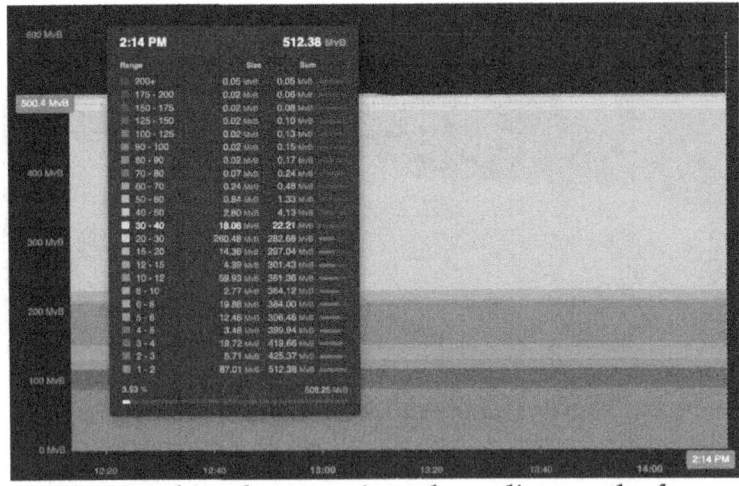

*Image: Number of transactions depending on the fee. The highlighted 30-40 sat/vB range has 18.08MvB and is 22.21 MvB from the "top".*

For example, if we sent a transaction with a fee of 30 sat/vB, we are 22.21MvB from the top, which means that if there were no other transactions paying that fee or more, it would take up to 23 blocks to be confirmed, which is an average of 230 minutes, or less than four hours. The problem is that transactions will keep coming in because many actors want to pay a fee per transaction that will cause a confirmation in the next block. The mempool.space site also visualizes this on the main page.

| No Priority | Low Priority | Medium Priority | High Priority |
|---|---|---|---|
| 45 sat/vB | 45 sat/vB | 49 sat/vB | 52 sat/vB |
| $2.71 | $2.71 | $2.95 | $3.13 |

*Image: Recommended fees from mempool.space based on priority. If you want confirmation in the next block, you should pay at least 52 sat/vB.*

So how much to pay? It is not a simple question, because we only know the current situation in the mempool and we do not know how it will evolve over time. There are various algorithms that can be used to predict confirmation within some time, but none is perfect. There are other algorithms besides the mempool.space algorithm, one of which can be found, for example, at light.oxt.me.

You may have noticed a dollar amount under the recommended fees. This of course depends on the value of the Bitcoin, but it is for a "normal" transaction, which is 140 vB. It doesn't depend on the amount you're sending, but on the size of the transaction in bytes.

Now imagine what happened to one of my friends - he accepted voluntary contributions to his project (also) through an on-chain transaction. That is, he had dozens of transactions to some of his addresses. Now, if he wanted to send those contributions all to an address, the transactions would have easily been a few kvB. For example, if he wanted to forward 100 voluntary contributions to a hardware wallet or to lightning, the transaction might be 17kvB. 17k*50=850k sat fee.

That's why, with on-chain payments, it's a good idea to consolidate transactions from time to time - that is, forward all payments to yourself at a time when fees are lower.

# I sent a transaction with too low a fee and it is unconfirmed for a long time

I stress that this is a situation you want to avoid. Most of the time when this happens to me, the result is hacking, copying private keys, and manually creating a transaction. But let's talk about some options anyway.

# Double spend, Replace by Fee

If we have sent a transaction with a low fee, we can simply make a new transaction. Thus, we spend the same coins twice ("double-spend"). In Bitcoin, the mechanism against double-spending the same coins is just mining, so if the transaction is not confirmed yet, it should be fine. And if it confirmed in the meanwhile, we don't have the problem with an unconfirmed transaction.

However, this runs into several practical problems. The first is the fact that not every wallet allows such a double-spend transaction to be easily created from its interface. And if it sees a transaction you've created in the wallet, it may not simply allow you to create another transaction with a higher fee.

This problem can be solved, for example, by importing the private keys into another wallet. Remember that Bitcoins are not actually in your wallet, the wallet is really a keychain - it contains private keys that allow you to create valid bitcoin transactions. Caution: Don't do this with Lightning wallets if you're not sure what you're doing, you might lose funds.

We can only make a replacement transaction if the wallet supports it. In addition, there is a special transaction flag called "replace by fee". If we look up the transaction using the block explorer at blockstream.info, we can see if Replace by fee is enabled for the transaction:

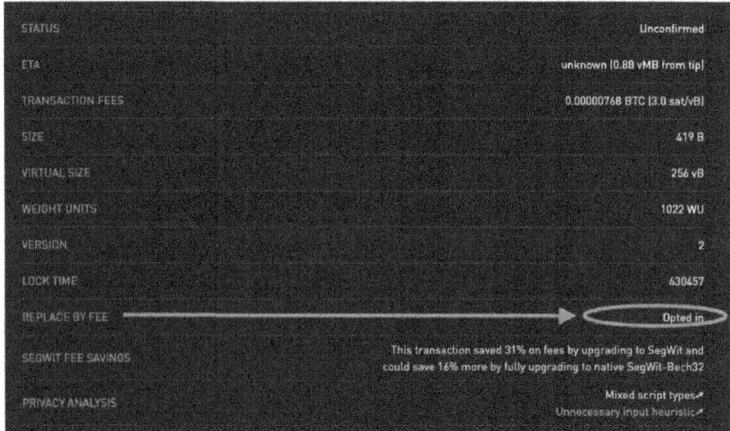

*Image: Looking at a transaction in some block explorers, you can see if they have the replace by fee flag enabled*

This flag is somewhat controversial and not binding. It tells Bitcoin nodes whether we want them to accept a replacement transaction with a higher fee into their mempool, if they already have another transaction that spends the original coins. It was meant to be a protection against double-spend attacks before the transaction is included in the block. However, what matters to the miner is whether the transaction is valid, and he is motivated to mine the highest-fee transaction. Thus, he may not care about any flags. At the same time, it is impossible to determine whether the miner respected the flag, because which transaction came first is determined by inclusion in the block; we cannot verify such information before confirmation, the nodes may have seen the transactions in different order!

Many nodes (including mine) run a Bitcoin core software with a setting that tells it to purposely ignore the replace-by-fee flag and allows the transaction to be replaced with one that pays a higher fee. This is partly so that application developers don't live under the confusion that the Bitcoin network would protect users from double spend attacks by other means than mining. Mostly, however, it is because the situation of a fee being too low and the user using a wallet that has not set this flag is common and users cannot cope with it easily otherwise.

*https://hackyourself.io/replace-by-fee*
*Watch video: Replace by Fee in Electrum wallet*

If your wallet supports it, you can usually create such a transaction by selecting this option in the menu.

## Child pays for parent

We can replace a transaction with another if we have the private keys and can sign the transaction. However, this may not be true in many cases. For example, if we have a pre-signed multisig transaction (such as closing of a Lightning channel), and we cannot "get hold of" or convince the other party to sign another transaction. A much more common case is that an unconfirmed transaction sends money to us, and we want to receive the money faster, not send it.

In this case, the recipient (and usually the sender) can do a "child pays for parent" transaction. This is the spending of unconfirmed coins back to their address. The fee must be high enough, so that the sum of the per-byte fees for both transactions is high enough to get the transaction into the block. If possible, some wallets (e.g. Electrum) allow you to create such a transaction directly from the menu - right click on the unconfirmed transaction and "Child pays for parent". The wallet will calculate what fee needs to be paid for the new transaction to go along with the old transaction the way we want it.

How to calculate it? If one transaction has, for example, 500 vB and a fee of 1 sat/vB and the second transaction will have, for example, 300 vB, what fee do we need to put on it so that on average both transactions will have a fee of, for example, 100 sat/vB?

Both transactions together have 800 vB. Together the fee should be *(100 sat/vB \* 800 vB)=80,000 sat*. In the first transaction we paid *(1 sat/vB \* 500 vB) = 500 sat*. So the new transaction fee must be 80000-500=79500 sat. The miner then looks at these transactions as a whole. He knows that if he wants to include the second one with the 79500 sat fee in the block, he must also mine the first one with the 300 sat fee. But it may still be worth it to him. The miners actually calculate the fees this way, so the process works.

https://hackyourself.io/child-pays-for-parent
*Video: Child pays for parent in Electrum wallet*

A minor problem arises if the lower fee transaction does not fit into the mempool as set by the miners. You need to send both transactions at the same time. If you receive such a transaction, it's a good idea to save it in hex format, as it's possible that your wallet will forget it too.

The receiver can always do this because he can spend the money coming in (to create a transaction that spends incoming money this transaction does not need to be confirmed, they can be included in the same block together).

The sender can only do this when there is a change that belongs to him. For example, if he sends 100,000 sat and spends an input of 100,500 sat, he has a single output of 100,000 sat. This happens relatively rarely, although the numbers may not exactly match. For example, if I want to send 101,000 sat to someone and I pay a 500 sat fee, it is not worth it to create another 500 sat output with a "change", because that will enlarge the transaction so that it will have more bytes and thus the total fees would be even higher. In addition, an output with a small value is practically unusable because the fee to spend it is higher than its value. In such a case, it is rational to either send the receiver a few extra sats or increase the transaction fee for the miners.

But if I have a transaction with a change output, I am also the recipient of the transaction (I receive the change). In that case, I can do exactly what the recipient did - spend the change as a not yet confirmed incoming payment, by creating a new transaction, and use the 'child pays for parent' strategy.

## Transaction Accelerator

Another option is to "bribe the miners" to include the transaction in the block despite the lower fee paid by the transaction itself. This means paying them in a way other than directly with a transaction fee, such as through Lightning - or even by a credit card (although that is quite lame). These services are often overpriced and I won't recommend them here. Google it if you really badly need it, but you won't be thrilled with the price. We'll see if there's competition pushing the prices down.

## Lightning network

In the previous section, we discussed how fees work in the Bitcoin network, what makes blockspace a scarce resource, and what to do if you've given too small a fee and the transaction is unconfirmed. Fortunately, paying a high fee is not the only and often not the best solution.

A common solution to the problem of fees is to use the Lightning network. However, it only works in certain circumstances. Let's take a look at when it pays off.

In Lightning, opening a channel (locking Bitcoins in a channel) is an on-chain transaction. We can then use the channel for as long as we like, and it's practically never worth closing it (if we need to make an on-chain payment, it's usually more convenient to use a swap service that securely sends on-chain coins after paying a lightning invoice).

If we send a lot of smaller payments, opening one channel and then using lightning payments will almost always save us money. With Lightning, there are fees, but they are not based on the size in bytes, but on the amount, and the percentages we pay are not high.

When receiving, we need to be careful about the capacity we can receive. If we have a channel to Bob, but all the coins in the channel ledger already belong to us, Bob can't send us any more coins through that channel. In that case, we need to either enlarge the channel (e.g. using splice-in technology like the Phoenix wallet does) or open a new channel. Both require an on-chain transaction.

Of course, it would be good to have a channel big enough to receive as much as we need. The Phoenix wallet provides this service (currently for a fee of 1% of the purchased capacity for a year and a mining fee to increase the channel). It's important to remember that Bitcoins locked in a channel are a scarce resource - someone must have them, and they're not locking them for us to use as we please for free.

The other option - especially if you run your own Lightning node - is to arrange with someone to open channels. The Lightningnetwork Plus service allows us to find counterparties to open triangles or polygons - Alice, Bob and Charlie agree to open channels together, for example at a rate of 1M sat. Alice opens a channel to Bob, Bob to Charlie and Charlie to Alice. All three will gain the capacity to send 1M sats as well as to receive 1M sats.

# Custodial lightning

The cheapest solution to the channel problem is custodial wallets. We can think of this as a bank account with a third party that allows us to receive and send money over the Lightning network. Custodial wallets do not meet the requirement of private ownership of Bitcoin - they are entirely dependent on the third party having "our" Bitcoins, allowing us to dispose of them. Thus, we trust that the third party won't get hacked or be attacked by some state regulation (this happens more often than one would think!).

Popular custodial wallet called "Wallet of Satoshi", for example, has removed its app from the Apple Store and Play Store from the US market in response to how they understand current US regulations.

**Wallet of Satoshi** ✓
@walletofsatoshi

To our valued Wallet of Satoshi community in the United States of America,

We've dedicated ourselves to providing the best Bitcoin experience with Wallet of Satoshi, being at the forefront of Lightning usability and adoption. However, we've made the difficult decision to remove our app from the U.S. Apple and Google app stores, and will not serve U.S. customers going forward.

This decision doesn't come lightly. Our commitment to providing a secure, user-friendly, and compliant platform globally is unwavering. Our top priority is the safety and interests of our customers and our company.

We understand this may be disappointing news and we share your frustration. We're hopeful that future developments will allow us to revisit and possibly resume our operations in the U.S.

For our existing users in the USA, rest assured that you have full access to your Bitcoin funds. You can seamlessly withdraw and transfer them to another wallet.

We deeply appreciate your support and understanding. We remain committed to bringing the benefits of Bitcoin to as many as possible.

Stay tuned for updates, and thank you for being a part of our community.

Peace, Love and Bitcoin,
The Wallet of Satoshi Team 💜

https://twitter.com/walletofsatoshi/status/1727937085741678679

*Image: Wallet of Satoshi's decision to remove the app from the App store and Play store in the US.*

Another popular wallet, Blue Wallet, has shut down Lightning's service to the public altogether. Personally, I don't think using custodial wallets makes much sense, but the low cost is undeniable - you don't have to worry about channels and thus don't make any onchain payments. The wallet operator handles everything for you. It also won't happen to you that you don't have the capacity to accept coins.

On the other hand, if you factor risk into the price, these wallets are only worth using for very small amounts.

## Uncle Jim

If we don't trust custodial wallet operators, we can go try for Uncle Jim. We all know and trust him. He runs his Lightning Node at his home datacenter in the basement, opens channels, monitors fees. There's no reason for everybody in the family to do that when Uncle Jim is dedicated to it.

Thus, by the "Uncle Jim" model we mean a custodial wallet, whereby we know the custodian personally, or it is someone in the family. For small payments this is often a really good solution. We can use this with lndhub in combination with BlueWallet, for example, or with the lnbits app. Later on, we will talk about other options based on e-cash platforms.

*Figure: Principle of operation of lndhub. The user interacts with the lndhub server, which does the accounting between users. It sends payments using a standard lightning node (lnd)*

Of course, we shouldn't always trust Uncle Jim either. But for small amounts, it's a good compromise - we don't have the risk of a large service that can be attacked by the state, and for hackers, Uncle Jim is also a smaller target. He should think about security, though.

# Non-custodial wallet

A very good solution is a non-custodial wallet that takes care of the channels. We have several options, the most popular are Breez, Phoenix, Blixt, Zeus, Mutiny Wallet. What does it mean that it takes care of the channels? It uses the services of a liquidity provider to open a channel (or increase the capacity of an existing channel). You can pay for liquidity directly when you receive it (Mutiny) or pay for it in the form of fees (Phoenix). Of course, you always pay fees to miners, so it's good to know how to work with channels. We'll cover this in detail in the next section.

Non-custodial wallets vary in restrictions, payment success rates, platform and the like. Phoenix Wallet, for example, is a fast unified balance wallet where you keep your balance in the Lightning channel but can still receive and send Lightning payments as well. The Mutiny wallet, for example, has separate on-chain and lightning balances - so you have more control over what channels you have open and what balance is in the channels.

Breez, like Phoenix, has a unified balance but runs a full routing node on your phone. You get better privacy and more control over your node at the cost of slightly slower payments (and if you don't use your wallet often, you'll have to wait for it to sync with the network from time to time). Phoenix lets you keep the private keys, but the server does the pathfinding for payment. This would normally be a problem since the server may expect too large fees, but in the case of Phoenix the fees are fixed - 0.4% of the outgoing payment.

Mutiny, Zeus and Blixt wallets allow you to open your own channels.

The popular Muun wallet does allow you to send and receive Lightning payments, but it's an on-chain wallet, so it won't help you save on fees.

## Permanent node

Another option, of course, is to use a custom node, with different front-ends. This option is for advanced users, but it doesn't necessarily mean you have to be a command line master. With projects like [Umbrel](Umbrel) you can have a lightning node, Nostr relay, Nextcloud, backup photos and do a few other things at home. At the same time, you can become Uncle Jim to your loved ones.

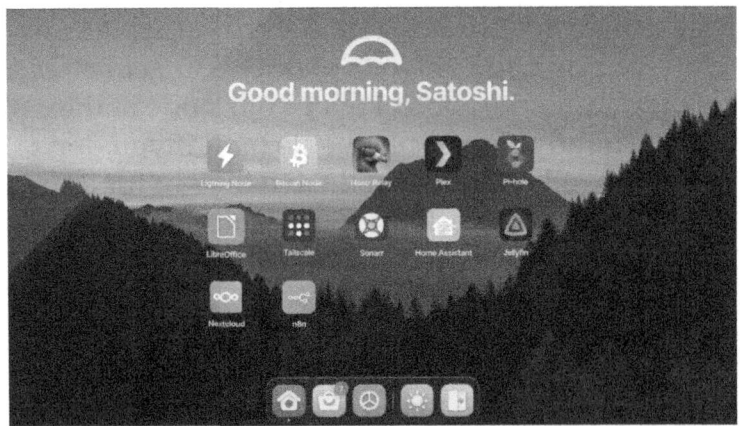

*Image: [Umbrel](#) Node Interface*

However, you need to take care of the channels - watch when the fees are low and use some of your bitcoins to open lightning channels.

# When are Lightning payments worth it?

Since we must open channels with Lightning, we won't get rid of on-chain fees completely. Depositing a larger amount of sats into a channel and making multiple small Lightning payments is the ideal use-case. To receive multiple smaller payments, we need to get hold of liquidity. This can be done by buying it or, for some wallets, by a simple trick – someone sends you a larger amount of bitcoins via Lightning (thus opening a channel for your non-custodial wallet) and you send some of the bitcoins back through lightning. You can receive the difference later over the same channel.

Of course, you can also get liquidity elsewhere, for example, you can arrange for three friends to open channels between you. One on-chain payment each and you're directly connected to the people you'll be exchanging Bitcoins with.

So Lightning is not for everything. For example, if you receive regularly, then without receiving capacity, increasing the channel will always cost an on-chain transaction (but you can buy liquidity). If you manage to create a larger on-chain channel, you will have a consolidated UTXO at the same time (recall that the on-chain fee is paid by size in bytes, so it's not good to have a lot of incoming on-chain transactions, as it can be expensive to spend them afterwards).

# Liquid

Liquid is a Bitcoin-like blockchain managed by a federation of custodians. It is possible to lock Bitcoins on the main bitcoin chain and get their representation (LBTC) on the Liquid chain. By being outside the bitcoin chain, Liquid can experiment a bit more with features. The basic differences are - different address format, confidential transactions (no visible amounts in transactions, like Monero), confidential assets (you can send tokens other than bitcoin, for example Tether – USDT - is popular). The way blocks are created is also different - these are confirmed by the federation and are created deterministically every minute. Even though transactions are larger, by being less used a transaction with a 0.1sat/vB fee currently gets into the block.

Unlike bitcoins locked in the Lightning network, liquid bitcoins are not bitcoins - you have to use an exchange service (such as [Boltz.exchange](Boltz.exchange)) or ask the federation to peg-in and peg-out to move them.

In a blog called "Expanding the Lightning network to serve billions – a quick win strategy" I suggested that with similar technology, the Lightning network could be extended without the need for trust to include channels that are backed by Bitcoins on Liquide. However, we are not there yet technologically. Right now, you can use Liquid with, for example, the Aqua or Blockstream Green wallets.

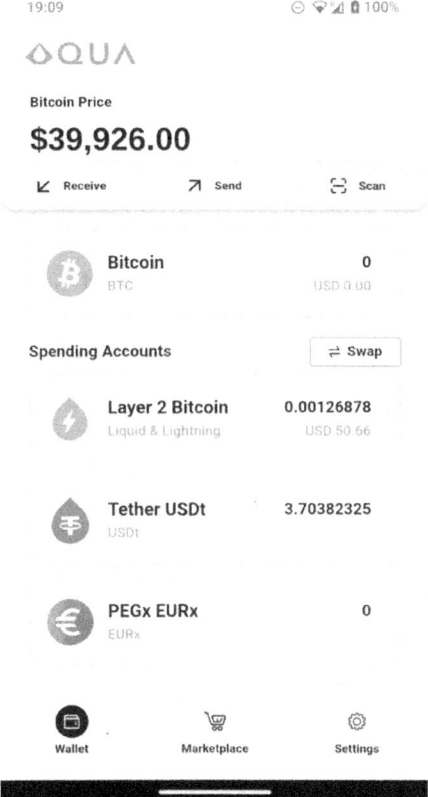

*Image: Aqua wallet interface*

Aqua also allows you to hold (and exchange) Tether (USDT) over Liquid. Additionally, it allows you to use your Liquid balance to pay a Lightning invoice using the swap service. From a user's perspective, this is something similar to the Muun wallet - while it's not a Lightning wallet, you should be able to accept and send Bitcoins via Lightning.

## Ecash - Cashu and Fedimint

Ecash (or Chaumian Ecash) is a method for making electronic cash that has been around since before Bitcoin. It is a completely anonymous method of making electronic cash. It uses so-called blind signatures. Let's try to imagine it like this. We generate a random serial number, write it on a denomination note (say 1000 sat). We go to the "mint", cover the serial number, pay the 1000 sat and get a stamp (signature) that guarantees that the note is valid. The mint does not see the serial number.

If we want to pay someone 1000 sat, we just need to send someone the serial number and signature. Either by text message, Signal, email or whatever. We can also display it in the form of a QR code. Of course, this is where the problem that Bitcoin solves with the blockchain comes in - how to ensure that someone doesn't spend this note twice, because the serial number has now been seen by two different people.

The e-cash system solves this by coming to the mint, showing the full serial number and signature. The mint recognizes a valid, signed note and puts the serial number on the list of invalidated notes (called spentbook) and confirms the new random serial number (adds a blind signature, but does not see the new serial number). The recipient of the original 1000 sat thus receives a new banknote whose serial number only he knows.

The interesting thing about this technology is that it does not create the transactions themselves - the transaction is the handing over of coins (notes) by text message. All that occurs is the exchange and invalidation of old coins. Since it is based on blind signatures, the Mint has no idea what coins have been spent or who they came from. It is thus a fully anonymous but centralized system.

Coins have different denominations (signed with different keys - stamped with different stamps), so there is another operation that is important – getting change. At any time I can go to the mint and ask for "change" for my 1000 sat, for example to get a 500 sat and 2x250 sat notes.

## Uncle Jim running an ecash mint

The more observant of you may have thought that the Mint might be run by Uncle Jim. This is exactly the idea of the Cashu project. And it's also related to Lightning. It is an e-cash system that is based on Bitcoin. You can also find various wallets online, a list of which is maintained by the main cashu.space site.

You can create Ecash tokens by paying a Lightning invoice created by the mint. Of course, you can send tokens to everyone who trusts the mint (for example, if you want to send money within your family) or just keep them in your wallet. If you want, you can use them to pay any Lightning invoice. Sending ecash is easy - either in terms of technical resources or liquidity and therefore transactions within a mint are mostly free.

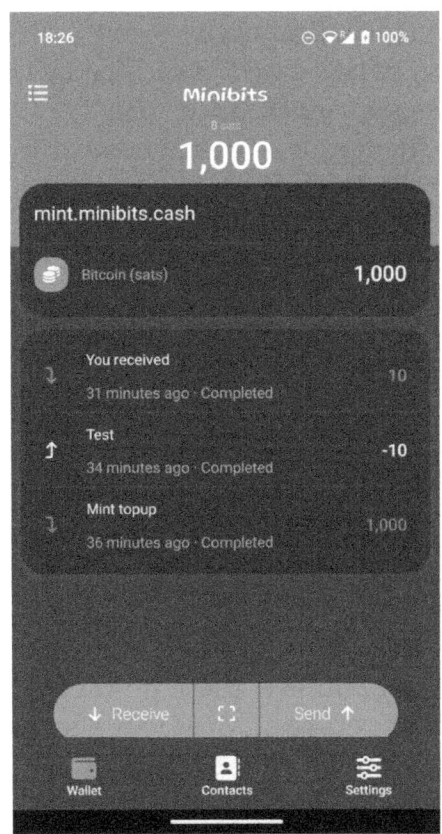

*Image. The <u>Minibits</u> wallet allows you to use multiple ecash mints from a nice Android app. There are also apps for iOS or the web.*

The advantage of this Uncle Jim model over lndhub or lnbits is that in this case Uncle Jim, as the mint operator, sees no user balances. He doesn't know who in the family is the richest, or if the nephew got some satoshi from his grandmother for his birthday. Despite this, the node is connected to lightning and allows all mint users to participate in the wider lightning economy. It's basically a version of a lightning wallet.

https://hackyourself.io/minibits-demo

*Video: Creating Minibits wallet (Android), recharging with Lightning, sending ecash tokens to cashu.me wallet.*

Maybe in some extended families, there might be more Uncle Jims - mint operators. Most wallets can work with multiple mints. And since they are connected by a lightning network, it is possible to move balances between them via the lightning network.

Another advantage of ecash is that it is very low data traffic and can therefore be run over LoRa, for example over the Reticulum network, as I show in this video:

https://hackyourself.io/nutband-demo

*Video: A look at how we can use the ecash cashu system over long range radio (LoRa).*

## Several Uncle Jims

Liquid solved Uncle Jim problem by trusting a federation of several people/companies instead of one person to trust. A similar model is used by an ecash mint called Fedimint. It is based <u>on the idea of federated ecash mints by Jonathan Logan and Frank Braun</u>. The idea is that instead of one mint, we have several and a blind signature must be added by a supermajority. The mints don't need to communicate with each other and they need to maintain their own spendbook each. This solution is also very fast and efficient, although mirroring the multisig setup in Lightning doesn't work so well - Lightning doesn't have multisig after all. However, there is a lightning gateway in the application.

https://hackyourself.io/fedi-demo

*Video: First look at the Fedi Alpha wallet*

Fedimint is in fairly early stages of development, you can use the protocol with Mutiny Wallet for example, but <u>the main community wallet Fedi</u> is still in beta and does not use mainnet coins as I write these lines. However, the authors are aiming to create a so-called "Superapp" in which users will have access to various services.

# Conclusion

What options do we have for using Bitcoin in a high-fee environment? We've shown how fees are determined, how we find out what the miners are currently asking for blockspace. We explained what to do if you sent a transaction with too small a fee.

Then we showed a few options - lightning network, with different types of wallets, liquid and ecash mints. Each of these options has different advantages and disadvantages. Some require trust (Uncle Jim and custodial options), some require some trust (Liquid), self-custodial lightning doesn't require trust, but you need to pay fees to open channels and get liquidity - if you are a regular Bitcoin user, this might not be a problem. If you want to onboard a family and just show people Bitcoin, ecash mints based solutions are perhaps better and allow payments over the lightning network. If you only want to do dollar cost averaging (i.e. mainly receive), a solution based on atomic swaps to Liquid, for example via the Aqua wallet, might be a good choice.

At the end of the day, it's mostly up to you and your needs, what fees you're willing to pay, and what's a priority for you.

With Bitcoin, the right tools can help you save on fees. In this chapter, you've learned about the options, now you just need to use them properly.

Made in the USA
Middletown, DE
04 January 2025

68825339R00119